THE NEW BLACK POETRY

THE

NEW BLACK POETRY

Edited with an Introduction

by CLARENCE MAJOR

INTERNATIONAL PUBLISHERS
New York

COPYRIGHT ACKNOWLEDGMENTS

The poems in this book are copyright by the authors, or their publishers, or representatives and may not be reprinted without their permission except by reviewers quoting passages in reviews. The biographical notes at the end of the book, which list the sources of the poems, are part of this copyright notice. In addition, thanks are due the following for permissions to use copyright material:

"W.W." by LeRoi Jones, copyright 1966, by LeRoi Jones; from *Black Arts,* permission by R. Hobbs, Literary Agent, New York. "I, Too, Know What I Am Not" by Bob Kaufman, copyright 1965, by Bob Kaufman, from *Solitudes Crowded With Loneliness;* reprinted by permission of New Directions Publishing Corp. "You Are The Brave" by Ray Patterson, copyright 1962 by the Hand and Flower Press, England; by permission of Ray Patterson. "I Looked & Saw History Caught," by A. B. Spellman, copyright by Hettie Jones; by permission of A. B. Spellman.

Library of Congress Catalog Card Number: 69–18879

Manufactured in the United States of America

I am the Smoke King.
I am black,
I am darkening with song,
I am hearkening to wrong;
I will be black as blackness can,
The blacker the mantle the mightier the man.

— W.E.B. Du Bois

ABOUT THE EDITOR

Clarence Major is 31 years old and lives and teaches creative writing in New York City. Born in Atlanta, Ga., he grew up and attended schools in Chicago, including the Art Institute. Author of the novel, *The All-Night Visitors,* he has also published three collections of poems, and has appeared in many anthologies, including *Black Voices* (New American Library), *In A Time of Revolution* (Random House), *The Writing On The Wall* (Doubleday). *American Negro Poetry* (Hill & Wang), *Where Is Vietnam* (Doubleday). He has also been widely published in the literary and poetry journals in this country as well as in Canada, India, Brazil and Mexico. Aside from teaching in Columbia University's Teachers & Writers Collaborative, the Academy of American Poets, the Harlem Education Program, Brooklyn College and elsewhere, he served two terms as writer-in-residence at the Pennsylvania Advancement School. He had read his poetry widely—at the International Poetry Forum, Carnegie Institute in Pittsburgh, the Guggenheim Museum, the Polytechnic Institute of Brooklyn, University of Nebraska, and the New School For Social Research, among many. He has edited his own literary journal, *Coercion Review* (1958-61), served as associate editor of a half dozen others, including book-review editor of *Anagogic and Paideumic Review,* and contributing editor of the *Journal Of Black Poetry.* He expects publication soon of a new collection of his poems, *The Sounds Of My Eyes.*

CONTENTS

ACKNOWLEDGEMENTS

Though, comparatively speaking, this has been a "one-man-project," I am thankful to my editor, James S. Allen, who introduced the idea for this book, Walter Lowenfels, Ishmael Reed, Lennox Raphael, Art Berger, and Welton Smith who read and commented on the poems during the early stages; to Hoyt Fuller and Nat Hentoff, who "advertised" it; to Dudley Randall, Russell Atkins, Wilmer Lucas, Paul Breman, Ishmael Reed, Art Berger, Al Young, David Henderson, Elton Hill, *et al.,* for supplying addresses of poets and spreading the "word"; to my wife, Sheila, who typed and typed until this projected material became the book that it is now; and of course to all the poets whose works form the contents.

C.M.

EDITOR'S INTRODUCTION

I

THE INNER crisis of black reality is often studded in these poems by the swift, vividly crucial facts and artifacts of social reality; which consists in part, anyway, of all the implications and forces of mass media, the social patterns, the bureaucratic and mechanical mediums of human perceptions, even of the quickly evolving nature of the human psyche in this highly homogenized culture, in all of its electric processes and specialist fragmentation. Black reality, in other words, is like any other reality profoundly effected by technology. The crisis and drama of the late 1960s overwhelms and threatens every crevice of human life on earth. These poems are born out of this tension.

I see our poems, social and political, as scientific new music: these constructs are solar concerts to the infinite tacit incantations of our elegance, as we are, as we long to be. Black radiance.

This is an elemental art of human communication (or vice versa) sweetly prodding the ornamented deadweight of *what* is left white folks from Greek, Roman equivalents. Our poems function like universal *mandalas* (circles) while they continually liberate our spirits. They are death cries to the pimp *par excellence* of the recent capitalist stages of the world, testimonies against the brutal psychological engravings of his base self-profit oriented psychology, his sham stance.

These poems speak the immortal language of symbolic and mystic love—the black power hissing is not only the cold blue nature of their pristine compassion but their drama: the firm way they educate.

Revolutionary art is always new. It achieves a classic stature instantly. Once standing in the governor's palace in Guadalajara, Mexico, looking straight up at Orozco's depiction of the "freeing of the slaves," this old truth became very clear to me. Like Siqueiros', his work reflects the quintessence of Mexican nationalism, those forms, ideas, people. The new black poetry, for very similar reasons, can usually be "experienced" clearly, anytime by anyone. We do not have to know what the daily life of an ancient Egyptian was like in order to "feel" the art he produced. Real art, no matter how unique, is never difficult.

Properly, we black poets in our unadorned passage through the sad cycles of life in these Western juxtapositions are aligned with the social and political struggles of visionary peoples who seek ultimately to renew the world, especially to authenticate this society.

Black poets here are practically and magically involved in collective efforts to trigger real social change, correction throughout the zones of this republic. We are mirrors here, and we know that anybody who has ultimate faith in the system is our enemy. Such people are obstacles. Our weapons are cultural, our poems. Like any concept, any art form, with an impetus in Afro-American nationalism, our poems exist primarily for and go directly to our central human needs, the people, our *shauku* (strong desire). Our minds are the strategy-drawing-boards of a social revolutionary battleground! Dragons breathing black fire! The experience of our "eyes," what the sounds of our spirits unearth...!

II

THE NEGLECTED and sometimes visciously suppressed real

history of our various forms of art before and since January 1, 1863, is a magnificent tragedy from *our* point of view. It includes all the music of our inner dwellings, from gospels to sophisticated beads of sound from John Coltrane to the iconoclastic poetry before us. The above date rings up the white concept of "Emancipation Day" as an historical reference, which is to us only a superficial fact in our continuous time from the genesis of our African spirit, rich in the way we (and all people, principally) come to ourselves as symbol.

This *kekima* (wisdom) has been personified vividly also here on the mainland since our appearance in Jamestown, Virginia, in 1619. We bring the ancient brilliance of the abstracts of black cultures, aesthetics—all the implied new distinct mythology, iconology, symbolism, etc., our submerged kingdoms, the black power of our cosmological armies, the horns of our virility, the tacit foresight of our acceptance of our past (the hardest thing for people to do), the spirit of our generations of collective positive durability—all of this into the skill, the tension and timing of the lines of these poems; which partly accounts for their separate and radical presence.

Out of the origin and growth of our creative song, the hieroglyphics of our enslaved bodies, bursting free, cracking open hot walls of time and space, we have as contemporary lessons this poetry as current history that is also another example of our precise undefaced cultural and human essence; as insignias these "songs" help to sustain our richness!

In the ancient past we have been giants of artistic scholarship; for example, much black poetry has the disposition of West African cultural abstracts. Our ancestors are freedom fighters like the writer Ahmed Baba of Timbuktu, in the fourteenth century.

Though we first came to North America as explorers

with Balboa, finding the Pacific and helping to establish Arizona and Mexico, to open the entire southwest, imperialist textbook-propaganda continues to distort and whitewash ugly and servile our past. And when the tone is not apologetic it is patronizing. But the presence of these poems encases the spirit of these facts we are relearning.

Out of the infinite *mandala* of human experience our art came finally ritualistically, from the economic origins of our captivity. We were such craftsmen as Jupiter Hammon and Gustavas Vassa. We shook this slaveholding nation with the fire of our words in the days of popular pamphleteering; the vigor of our natural wisdom shot through the English language, awakening the biologically asleep; and the intellectual and egocentric white liberal hearts suddenly *had* to be concerned, to see us as human: which quickly contradicted every principle the nation was built on.

Meanwhile the circle of our spiritual orientation was a stabilizing force for any and every division of our folkloric black culture. However, in the contradictions of our presence grew our gods, arts, politics, nationhood-sense; and the spirit of this movement continues, radically opposed to any alienation from the community.

Through our projectives came our percussive or prospective art forms. The syllables of our eyes, the speech music of our black church, the work song of our hammering dogma, the perceptions of our ears.

While the poets of the slaveholding class were still snowed (imitators) inheritors of Chaucer and all that England was when it was still part of Europe, the black American poets, though also doing derivative work, were somewhere else. It is very simple: Phillis Wheatley, a slave girl, wrote better poems than Longfellow. Paul Laurence Dunbar's artificiality is less artificial than Emily Dickinson's.

[14]

III

W.E.B. Du BOIS precisely understood the validity of Afro-American poetry when in 1903 he wrote, in *Souls of Black Folk,* "by fateful chance, the Negro folk-song stands today not simply as the sole American music, but as the most beautiful expression of human experience born this side of the seas...the singular spiritual heritage of the nation and the greatest gift of the Negro people."

Conscious of this black poets are using every ounce of *uganga* (native medicine) available to win a firm reality for the spirit of nationhood, and ultimately the spirit of brotherhood. The *uganga,* for some, is the means to the structure of black consciousness. Needless to say, revolutionary black poets feel the urgency of being in a political vanguard. As a matter of fact, many of these poets are full-time militant activists. Any droopy concepts of western ideology are already obsolete. Even the best radical white poets today are beginning to question the whole western cultural aesthetic.

What cannot be stressed too often is that the social and political situations that house the spirit out of which this new angry love poetry flows are decorated with dead relics. The capitalist imperialist Euro-American cultural sensibility has proven itself to be essentially anti-human and is being rejected not only by black poets—black people—but also by the white artist, the white radical activist. The structure stifles free human will; the oppressor's vision of the world even hampers his own humanity and drags him despite himself into the butt-end of the survival question of contemporary experience.

So the black artist or writer and his allies, demanding of themselves a fuller consciousness, are forging a transformation of ethical-aesthetic proportions paralleling the radical political changes in the society—in the world, as a matter of

[15]

fact. We know that without a new, radical and black aesthetic the future of black people shall be empty. The progress of this new vision of the world, a black vision, broadens and deepens the beauty of this nation, of the world. The only really unfortunate aspect of the whole situation is that the dominant white society has been brainwashed into seeing the black upheaval as a negative force. No matter what happens the misfortune shall be a white misfortune. Nobody has told America more eloquently than black poets how it can save itself, but America is deaf.

This assessment may sound harsh against the mechanical specialist culture, the electric speed of data processing—that kind of virture, I mean, IBM precision, and so on. Let me say, I appreciate the strides of technology but not when they are *made in exchange* for the full realization of whole thoughts and whole feelings of human beings. This capital-istic slave-system society has suddenly found itself pitched headlong into the space age, and is staggered and dumb-founded: our entity poems are works hammering this chaos into ethical forms, like metal sculpture.

The importance of culture—or specifically poetry—in black self-determination cannot be underestimated. Despite grow-ing white suppression (superior weapons), black people, in our sense of culture, remain filled with positive images and voices, to say the least. When I watch the gentle beauty of Ruby Dee's face, or listen to the stammering articulation of James Baldwin, or witness the gentle anger in Nina Simone's voice, this upbeat spirit becomes profoundly clear. There is no decadence and inanity in these poets. Black poets are not escapist no matter how stale their lives may be.

Yes; we bring to American literature a positive radical alternative to its present emptiness at a time when most white American writers are not being honest with themselves.

We are getting back to the true spirit of things and in line with this operation the oppressed poet's selfhood can be measured precisely by the degree of destructive energy he exacts against symbols of or the oppressor himself: for the good of all. Our situation is an example. Like students burning down buildings that *lie* to them, our poems aim ultimately to help deliver the capitalist oppressive system to some museum of time, to leave it "out there" somewhere as a relic of western space.

IV

WALTER LOWENFELS said to me, "There's worse racism in poetry publishing than in the Plumbers' Union or National Association of Manufacturers. It's almost impossible for a black poet to get a book published over here. Furthermore, when I hit at this racism in my anthologies or talks, it runs off the backs of liberals as if they were made of shark skin. We each have to find our own way of fighting racism through our own craft....Black poetry is written in English and cannot help but be part of the North American creative scene." (Lowenfels assembled in 1964, the first USA poetry anthology that contained a fair—20 out of 85—sample of work by black poets: *Poets Of Today,* International.) He wrote: "The overall failure of white readers, critics, teachers, anthologists to recognize the role of the black poet in the image of American literature is part of the overall white refusal to recognize the image of Afro-American life. Because it is in essence their national spirit that finds expression in Afro-American poetry." ("Black Renaissance," *American Dialogue,* Summer 1968.)

And from the *New York Times,* March 6, 1968: "Lowenfels emphasized in his talk that poetry ought to have a strong social character and suggested that the most important force in American poetry today was the poetry of social protest by young Negroes."

And it *is* true. When I first started publishing poetry in 1958 several journals, some located in the South, printed my work without realizing I am black and their editors later experienced deep frustration when this incidental information came their way. But this didn't worry me then, and it doesn't worry me now. Like most other black poets, indeed, like the radical revolutionary poets of the world, I am somewhere else.

V

OUR POETRY is shaped by our experience in the world, both deeply personal and social. Unlike most contemporary white poets we are profoundly conscious of forces that ironically protect us from the empty patterns of intellectual gentility and individualism, and at the same time keep our approach fresh. We constantly mean our poems to reshape the world; in this sense, all excellent art is social; the proper movement of human art is to shatter illusion and make concrete the most explicit and useful reality.

Some parallels of our poetry today are experienced in advertising and other media but more significantly in the song stylings and instrumentations of John Coltrane, Pharoah Sanders, James Brown, Aretha Franklin, Wilson Pickett, Sam Cooke, Sun Ra, Cecil Taylor, Ray Charles, *et al.* This is the essential energy that is blackness, the lyricism of this consciousness. The *beat* as opposed to anything melodic. These voices, sounds, this mysticism: a kind of underground creative mixed-media biography of the most spiritually-oriented life in North America.

From it we have automatically invented a new means of seeing. We have given a clarity, a freshness to English: a new turn, a vivid life. Our language is born of sound clusters, as opposed to Shakespeare's, which derives from the nexus, *sight*.

These poems are tools of black power, coming freshly from the community-spirit; they educate, reeducate. They automatically assume their cultural responsibility, their momentum is our feeling but can be anybody's way of correcting the stagnant myths men often fall victim to. (That is not to say that there are not myths here—but they are functional, like tools). The United States is like a chicken that can't fly but has wings. Human life sustains a large part of its essence through the symbolic use of myths and while human societies always evolve, the most ideal mythology does not often correlate. This is what white America does: carry wings (myths) that are useless; or more precisely, dangerous. The blue-blood, anti-intellectual love of Paul Bunyon, the Lone Ranger, Superman, Billy The Kid, etc., is symptomatic proof. Poems such as ours are self-defense bullets to puncture the immodest formation of any corruption *from them* that rubs off on us—which, because of the way society is organized, *does* happen.

VI

MOST ANTHOLOGIES of American poetry have been compiled either along lineal or historical lines; but the contextual definition of this volume is more cultural than racial; and many anthologies, as LeRoi Jones points out, are "taste-manuals," or, in any case, a reflection of who and what the editor is. Lowenfels states that his anthologies are "statements," forms of literary criticism in themselves. The dead-weight of those anthologies of so-called contemporary Negro American poetry put out by people like Arna Bontemps and Langston Hughes has done nothing but mislead a lot of white folks; for the most part, black readers have known for

[19]

a long time that Paul Laurence Dunbar is not a contemporary poet. And Rosey E. Pool's anthologies sound just a little too patronizing.

Approximately one fourth of the creative writers I initially solicited responded, and the work here represents about the same percentage of what was submitted; but at least again as many (76) equally gifted Afro-American poets active today might have been selected.

A considerable percentage of these poets have not published anywhere previously.

In collecting these poems, my primary concern has been, first, with the artistic quality of the work, and second, with the *quantity* of the poets' social black consciousness, i.e., the degree to which IT is intrinsic to the human quality of the poem.

Though none of these factors were selectivity determinators, only about ten of us were born before 1930; the largest percentage were born from about the middle of the Depression (1932) to the end of World War II (1945); several of us were born *since* 1945. At this writing, only two of the poets are deceased—Rivers and Durem. Though I have made no attempt to exploit a geographical diversification in reference to the poets selected, they came from almost every section of the nation, and even beyond the motherland.

For the first time in *any* anthology, to my knowledge, here is a fair representation of female poets; and, as a matter of fact, this is the first truly black anthology of *its kind* to be published in the United States.

It may be clear that black schools of *vital* poets are at the peak or swiftly reaching the peak of artistic fertility. Out of this passionate social consciousness the course of world literature is being reshaped and led in an entirely new direction. Here in the motherland we see evidence of the black arts movement spreading from Harlem to the West Coast, Detroit,

Cleveland, Philadelphia, Newark, Washington, D. C.; with the black student *mojo* movement on the campuses of Fisk University, Columbia University, Hunter College (New York), San Francisco State College, Lincoln University, Oberlin College, Wilberforce College (Ohio); black writers workshops are springing up everywhere, not just in Watts and Cleveland, in New York and Detroit!

More and more anthologies like this will appear—because this renaissance has an unmistakable international spirit! Examples: in Cuba, brilliant poets like Nicholas Guillen, Miguel Barnet, Luis Suardiaz; all through South America, poets like Otto Rene Castillo and Ernesto Cardenal; black poets like Jacque Roumain of Haiti, Aime Cesaire of Martinique, Jorge de Lima of Brazil, are engaged also in defining and reshaping world literature along revolutionary and socialist lines. In our own country the furious and inventive excitement, however, equals the fermentation anywhere. And the fruit of this spirit shall be heard in the world, suppression notwithstanding.

New York City   —CLARENCE MAJOR
September 1968

THE NEW BLACK POETRY

S. E. ANDERSON

A New Dance

And there they were: with fire everywhere
brothers instantly bonded for life
for life
and there was fire everywhere:
in their hearts, in their eyes, in their shackhomes

But burn they must
and burn we must

Black is the spiralfire through corridors
of white halls enflaming

The white one must be cremated to be saved
and we must cremate to be saved

It will not be burning black streets
It will not be our burning homes
It will be the downtowns of ofayclowns
honking their pallid tunes across
this stolen land

       and we dance the Blackflame dance
       in tune to the rhythm of our times

We rebegin where our brothers began:
cleansing-fire spreads from city to city
to country to country
to world

and we dance the Blackflame dance
in tune to the rhythm of our times

to be alive for the world to be alive
we dance the Blackflame dance
we will
we are—

watch us....   ..join us.

RUSSELL ATKINS

Editorial Poem On An Incident

Of Effects Far-Reaching

All who have and have all can cry: "PEACE!"
All who have not may despair to war.
And so M. Mallory believed in this:
Having the most less is not having more!
Be content with vacant, abstract power?
with hollow and alack and futile sacrifice
for which no trophy may be given ever?
Why waste into eternity at this price?
I'd experience a courage of as mad
and profound as this due M. Mallory!
She requires a compassion huge but sad:
Justly, hers was a war's philosophy.

"Power! True, natural power!" is advised.
Legal angles can not nor can "education"
Fashion a race a cosmic dignity that thrives!
(Time is cruel and nation kills nation!)

An M. Mallory knows who comes with doom,
Whose army, whose police gather and why.
A vigilance is hers for from a "moon"
more enslavement's bred in the sky.

She entertains no fool's fantasy of power
to be absolved as worlds turn wise.
Many a Mae Mallory stirs the hour:
Weak councilmen must decide by and by.
Theirs is what *hope* in another's historics?
"Fame" as "negro" councilmen at delegations?
What's their *might* in another's politics?
Their opinions? Who dominates decision?

I would not wish to have reflected hope
from City Hall be clearly shone before,
then drear'd upon by judicial gloom
fade with shade of shutting doors,
or hear a hush of over-and-done-with
after they would've made reports of me,
waved me in air, crammed me in briefcases,
typewritten me but set nothing free!

Will train with its knelling bell, loom up?
wheels with a prison's clangor groan farewell?
Will distance, night and forever enwrap
M. Mallory? Is Monroe her hell?
Were I someone to be placed living
on a death of train horror'd through dark or day
I would have the feeling of brave—but,
sitting in a rolling grave!

Where taken from the train—what wold?
Beyond community perhaps, where distant light's

no help? Will courtroom sanctuary hold
(should angels—or devils—keep a soul safe)
or will "justice" *too soon* leave the clerk
closing up after an "over" and shut case?
Oh how from deep, from righteous, from humane
can logical compassion sudden up?
at logic some compassion wanes:
at compassion some logic stops!

LAWRENCE BENFORD

The Beginning Of A Long Poem

On Why I Burned The City

My city slept
Through my growing up in hate
Bubbling in the back streets.
The sun shone on my city
But curved not its rays back
Into the corners where I shined shoes
With my teeth,
Where my father ate the trash of my city
With his hands,
Where my mother cared for white babies
With black breasts.
My city, yes, outstretched along
Its white freeways slept
In the warmth of its tall new building
And 100000 $ homes
Of abnormal sapiens with titles

—And I grew up!

Like a wild beast awaking
To find his mate eaten
In one second I grew up
With the fires that flamed
In my soul. Fires that burned
Holes in the soft spots of my heart.
(So as not to bleed to death)
They were plugged with lead
And I went off to college
With a Gasoline can.

LEBERT BETHUNE

To Strike For Night

The man with the blood in his sight
with the knife in his voice
and nothing to lose but that life
which in living like them
comes to death—is me
The man with the children on fire
his women with panthers for titties
and something to hate like that love
which in loving like them
comes to nothing but death—is me
The man who will win is me
the man who cant die anymore
the man who forged behind patience and smiles
a long black gun of justice
that man is me
I'm Dedan
I'm Toussaint, I'm Garvey
I'm names that in dying for life

make life surer than death
Yes
The man with the blade poised
to strike for my night
That black man is me.

HART LEROI BIBBS

Six Sunday

O Tremble! O Tremble, O Tremble.
Shook with Government dynamite was a true faith.
In D.C., on the twenty-eighth laughingly given as
                                        lambs
Young brothers and sisters this was your freedom.
Hymned you the while old American songs?
"My country tis of thee sweet land of slavery."
Foreign fights are no longer your wars;
At home is where freedom must ring
For unpurposeless men in Birmingham do
                                        children die
Protesting laughing, shuffling non-parental
                                        meekness.
How can we fight they cry, what have we?
Machine guns have with spears been jammed;
By human hands, like cockroaches, lions been
                                        crushed.
Aah! the blood—from six sunday blood spattered
So die you shall even on the holy day
Confirmed by your host the white God little it
                                        mattered
For even is the number of horror of His everyday.
It chokes the nostrils of cowards.

[28]

AUSTIN BLACK

Soul

from ivory towers they come
for poetry music art & food
no homosapien peers for you
grand delusion's soul supreme
funky soul brothers keeping the faith
gleaned from squalid shambles of life
      400 years of crass illusion
great soul erotic soul happy soul
your splashed canvas expensive now!
preserved cans to tickle the palate
      stored bottled crated you see
pressed in wax in sharps & flats
      hours days seasons & years
soul the pain of misery amassed!
depriving altars of physical joys
      philosophy of being in the void
for soul is where its really been
      faded thin hand-me-downs
just simply take a look inside
      eating funky souled ghoulash
from disconcerted spiritual void
      the individual striving suicide
      wisdom of age is not facade!!!

EDWIN BROOKS

Tulips From Their Blood

I

Dear murdered Comrades, not in vain
your red blood paints this earth;
we lock the xiphoid killers in coffins,

II

we boogie-woogie and do zigankas in Nat Turner's Jubliees,
no men, with heads of lions, eat people;
to Vietnameses we give a kiss of peace,
doves hover-fly the metagalaxy,
virtue conjugates multiplication,
a woman leads the nations
Martin Luther King, Jr. is President,
your zendik children trigger computer-factories,
they lasso plasma and corral the generations of atoms,
flamingo Beethovens vibrate from the brains of workers,
binary sonnetizes Shelley,
ten decennaries they live
cameras catechize precision movements,
they throw the gauntlet at death,
sonic scalpels pliant for a doctor-engineer,
refrigerator houses store hearts and brains,
disease lies dead,
memories, like potatoes, are transplanted;
in hums of electricity they sleep three hours,
they converse with precambrian,
laser fingers hound infinity
they carry libraries in a briefcase, and

television sets in the palms of their hands,
pears big as cantaloupes,
wheat and trains root-fast in tundras,
whale farms swim seas,
they cartographize floors of waters,
the lift up Andrea Doria,
their hologram-eyes telescope the inner core
they hide people from furies of earthquakes,
they shall wrestle with zero
robots create window-homes revolving after the sun,
cybernetics in the basement,
driverless cars zip-zap elevated highways,
moving sidewalks taxi pedestrians,
only conveyors load trucks,
miners never descending extract diamonds,
exploders jet-ram tunnels through mountains,
bores bite the deepest ocean's bottoms,
explorers map unknown Venezuelas, and
man-made suns and cities hang from the sky,
they make it rain,
Osceola and Caocooches crack protein codes,

III

purple grapes scent desert bins,
glass skyscrapers punctuate centillion light-year births
Of photon-jets bannering your martyred name.

F. J. BRYANT

The Languages We Are

The stacked houses on either side
Of ours hold up the walls that form our rooms.
We drape our windows with our selves
And watch the parade below. Inside,
As clean as the poor can be, we speak
The languages we are forgetting
The thin wall's ears.

Our home shrouds us with its ribs
Showing and protects us from rain
Though we spot the floor with pan barrels.
In Summer it boils our energy.
We vary between in Fall and Spring.
But, in the Winter...
Oh, in the Winter...
We cling to our frosty vapors and
Melt it with hate-heat eyes for warmth.

ED BULLINS

When Slavery Seems Sweet

When slavery seems sweet
its scent is Chanel
and rustles Sachs silk
upon an ivory slide
that presses
your Black balls
like Burgundy grape

When slavery seems sweet
it wakes you with a
listerine kiss
& sends you to the
corner to its father,
Saul
(six eggs
your morning meal,
dear)
& please don't read
the paper before coffee,
darling,
you know how the
news of Mississippi
gets you up on the
wrong side of the
morning

When slavery seems sweet
it has a history
buried in the caves of
Germany, Russia, Poland,
Great Britain...and re-
members a grandfather, a
junk peddler,
in St. Louis,
spoke nothing 'cept
Yiddish

When slavery seems sweet
You wallow within
its colorless
flesh, seep through
its skin

(a slug, you are)
your eyeball sweating
hate of yourself
& when you come
inside that form
you scream & dream
of the creamy Eunuchs
that will one
day noose the barbed
wire about
your Black throat...

  singing
  daddy
  daddy
  daddy

LEN CHANDLER

I Would Be A Painter Most Of All

for peter lafarge

i am here again
pox marks have obscured my dimples
i smile most now when standing on my head
  (or appear to)
i think best upside out
or inside down

MY EYES WERE
once bright wholly holy eyes
  for looking out and looking in

my eyes were spying periscopes
        for peeping up and over
for looking around corners
        (most of mine and some of yours)
without exposing my head
        my neck was very short then
        and easy to keep in
        (giraffes don't need periscopes)

wide eyed and boy scout young
i stood close to the fire soon
early evening...campfire heat
wind smoke and cinders
narrowed eyes to slivers
first to carry wood
first to fetch the tinder
first to strike the match
and fire the fire
on the inner edge of circle
staring in...with eyes wide open
looking at the backs of others
standing backs to fire
far from fire and ash and cinder
staring in the black of forest
caring not for log nor ember
fond of eyes and faces
and the sound of their own voices

and i with eyes unblinking
SEEING
        only fire and ash—and
HEARING
        only chorus of wind and fire—and

FEELING
>only heat and tingle—and

SMELLING
>only smoke of pine and

TASTING
>only promises of potatoes
>wrapped in leaves...and packed
>with mud and

TOUCHING
>all the secret places of
>fire and light and energy...and

KNOWING
>nothing but guessing...almost
>every all

riding in the open truck
>going home from summer camp

seeing still the fire consuming
log and branch and twig and tinder
as if it had seared its signal
on the back of these eyes
that i had used as whetstone
for the edge i still most hone
to cut through my unknowing
in that open truck through woods
remembering smell and all
between the senses that were cited
only as a milestone...
though i'd measured with micrometer
each was tangled in the total
my eyes were wide and open then
seeing clearly all the edges
i was riding facing front
the rest were looking back
i knew where i had been

i was looking at the black bird
when a low limb caught my eye
flooding chest with antiseptic tears
        red and feigning fire
        (perhaps not feigning for
        some of it was consumed)
i was nine then...at nineteen i got glasses
i was just the other side of ten
when first i learned
how soft the edges are
when things are just
a little out of focus
unfocus the billboard
and the ad man has no dominion
unfocus...and the razor edge
seems less sharp
i know it now to be
the day i started going blind
i know it now to be
the day i started going blind
the day i discovered
it was easier not to see
i let my eyes unfocus more and more
i found comfort in the haze
walking toward an almost shadow world
only really looking at what i had to

i learned to squint my ears
and to unfocus words
and   reduce to tempo and pitch
        all their meaning
i learned to love abstractions young
to squint in all my senses
to shadow dream think

to drift around soft edges
to squint my skin
to feel little
to heal fast

had i held to blindness
i would have held to life
i would have been a pure musician
laying easy dot on line
in time and tempo—safe
safe—for a world of Wallace's
or l.b.j's. could see me as
no real or present danger
they might even tap their heel
(u.s. steel cleats and all)
—don't make the tyrant
tap his heel when his
foot is on your neck

had i held to blindness
i would have been a poet
surrounded by a hedge
of literary illusions
and read by those few
who have the biggest purse to pay
and reason to find comfort in
the totally obscure

but now i dare see clearly as a child
and now i even almost understand
now i would be a painter most of all
my medium would be
words and color and shape
and shape and texture

and smell and time and taste
i would press my picture
to the back of your brain
for you too have learned
to squint in all your senses
    so i must enter where i can
and hang my pictures
where you dare not even blink

SAM CORNISH

To A Single Shadow Without Pity

you are all these people
and will die soon they wade
in the filth of my mind
with tender feet extend
through my fingers with a quiet
uncertain voice each face
reflecting the greys
of small compromise
i live somewhere in the lines
in their faces and cannot convince
them of my intentions there is some
meaning on the hesitation
of a lip the quick
of the eye learning
the description of a different
street when it sees you
on a sudden corner where my
eyes will not let them alone

from all the minutes i am pushed from
where i hear music they do not understand
i wish there could be a silence of them
behind their faces i wish we could never
think of speaking behind these faces
without this music learning itself
within me
not knowing how to die
without music can be pain
unless you are someone who
understands all you want
is only sleep
and the music
touching the blankness
in the spaces where
the body hurts

not knowing how to die
i find myself in music
because the fingers
extend only the lies
of your own mind
my obscure words
too much like yours
where there is walking
in this city drinks a
dull mind

not knowing how to listen
because so many stone
structures are dead
with exhaustion
not wanting to die
because the fingers

want to extend themselves
i constantly feel
rhythm
we are drifting westward
where no landmarks are visible

the earth turns
on the edge
of the plow

red house
near the bridge
a corpse came home
& went to sleep

crows
on distant fences
near the river
cannot mourn

eyes have turned
to stone
white
except the trees
the sky almost
reaches the red
house
almost touches
his hands

        under the trees
        the stone and you
        shall go no further

under the trees
the flowers sleep
with memory

you will feel
no more winter
branches will spread

and you
feel no more

STANLEY CROUCH

Chops Are Flyin

> *Chops are flyin everywhere*
> *and there's nothin* says Louis
> *but old Duke left in there.*
> *Get away, Duke, get away!*

Get away, they're all gone
way up to what's beautiful
all the older men
mellowed down lower than new flowers

but flowers are not animal enough
to illustrate the beauty of these men
who are graceful as summer
as the warm would be aged
were it buried within
a body to then
glow through it,
blood bent backward

and bursting, straight,
up to God
hit Him right between the eyes
and make Him smile

Yes, it is that they speak
and what they have to say
is unreasonable
because of what they are
to have been this black
like the casted shape of a great spirit
under the bars of this mad
and savage place—tipped
where the only singing many times
was the whistling of a buckeyed
body adangle like a grotesque
blossom from some tree

Slaves anyway but never
emasculated is what these
men say to me
though some stumble upstairs
under alcohol—
half dollar bottles of dark port
or three times that much
for some kind of whiskey,
buried like kings
in pyramids of flophouses
their deeds rotted
from the minds of the people
on the street—
                    or even
like beautiful of the half valve Boy Meets Horn Rex
who had in his last days

a job on a jive
magazine *writing*
about music
or asking an untalented critic
if he could get a job
as a waiter in a club
just to be near it

barrels of bullshit
have been the quicksand
these men have had to wade through
only so that they could continue
to be beautiful
But no beauty is wanted
here none at all, never

Never, but these men standing
tall, giants maybe
will always be this way. Trees
whose height we can climb
just listening, to sit there
our legs swung over the branches of their deeds
able with no difficulty to see
far beyond the smoke, the buildings
and the terror of these cities
just as Duke has said
"When everything else is gone
the music,
                    will still be here"

VICTOR HERNANDEZ CRUZ

Urban Dream

1

there was fire & the people were yelling. running crazy
screaming & falling. moving up side down. there was fire.
fires. & more fires. & walls caving to the ground   & mercy
mercy. death. bodies falling down. under bottles flying in
the air. garbage cans going up against windows. a car singing
brightly a blue flame. a snatch. a snag. sounds of bombs.
& other things blowing up.
times square
electrified. burned. smashed. stomped
hey over there
hey you. where you going.
no walking. no. running. no standing.
STOP
you crazy. running. stick
this stick up your eyes. pull your heart out
hey.

2

after noise. comes silence. after brightness (or great big
flames) comes darkness. goes with whispering. (even soft
music can be heard) even lips smacking. foots stepping all
over bones & ashes, all over blood & broken lips that left
their head somewhere else, all over livers, & bright white
skulls with hair on them. standing over a river watching
hamburgers floating by. steak with teeth in them. flags.
& chairs. & beds. & golf sets. & mickey mouse broken
in half governors & mayors step out the show. they split.

3

dancing arrives.
like in planes. like in cars.
yes. yes. yeah. mucho boo-ga loo. mucho.
& sections of land sail away. & suicide rises. idiots jumping
into fires. the brothers five sing the blues as they sink. kids
blow their brains out, first take glue, & then shoot their
skull caps off, with elephant guns.

& someone sings & someone laughs. & nobody knows.
& chant to gods.
& chant to gods.

alarm clock bursts.

GLORIA DAVIS

To Egypt

Where are my people?
When will your tales unfurl,
            and let the white world know
You were once my mother
and I
your soft kinky headed girl...
Tell them—
White America, I mean,
How you built me a strong black nation
            from a vibrant black seed!
Tell them that my fathers,
            the Pharaohs, were black.
Tell the white world

let them know Hannibal,
   was my brother.
And that the temples soothed in blackness
were the toys of a
foolish girl.

R A Y   D U R E M

Problem In Social Geometry—

The Inverted Square!

for Ferlinghetti

I have seen the smallest minds of my generation
assume the world ends at Ellis Island.
that its capitol is North Beach,
and Fillmore is a nightown Street
for weary intellectuals.

Man, there were no hypes at Stalingrad,
and Malcolm X is real!
Spare us the cavils of the nihilistic beats
who criticize the cavities and contours of their nest,
but never leave it.
Warm in its filth,
maggots in a rotten apple
with their little pens or paintbrush
They deride the filth they feed on,
they flutter but they never fly.

Little beat bearded Bohemian brother
There are capitols in this universe
beyond your bagel shops and book stores;

Bandung was no chimera, nor Cairo
you think we are so different from Egyptians?
or those in Tres Marias with Zapata?
Bird sang sweet, but sweeter is the song of La Habana
and its echo deep in Monroe County
swings, man, and you are not with it

Man, like,

When you tire of pot
Try thought.

HARRY EDWARDS

How To Change The U.S.A.

From an interview New York Times, *May 12, 1968*

For openers, the Federal Government
          the honkies, the pigs in blue
must go down South
          and take those crackers out of bed,
the crackers who blew up
          those four little girls
in that Birmingham church,
          those crackers who murdered
Medgar Evars and killed
          the three civil rights workers—
they must pull them out of bed
          and kill them with axes
in the middle of the street.
          Chop them up with dull axes.
          Slowly.

At high noon.
        With everybody watching
on television.
        Just as a gesture
of good faith.

JULIA FIELDS

Black Students

In groves of green trees
The world is pastoral and
Through green fields of innocence
You walk in quiet bucolic splendor
Thinking life will make some salutation
To a pink or gold card bearing the alphabet
Through A B C D E F or S and I.
You await the fall
And the X-Ball.

You learn to sip your tea—
The little brownie turned, absurd, just so,
And how to appreciate Wedgewood
And Chippendale, thinking Benin is a kind of gin
Hoping to see the Great Nations of Europe
And photograph the stately ruins there.
Africa is an ambassador with nappy hair.
A magazine rack erupts in your room
And bulges with the offerings from Look, Life,
Time, Newsweek and the Readers Indigestion.
One lone case of white Encyclopedia Britannica stands
Untouched, But there is no picture of Christ hanging

With Messianic, tortured blue eyes
Muttering "I's lynched, I dies."

One therefore assumes a sort of progress has been made
Though the brains are intact
Fresh as the thoughts of the newly born
With no puzzlement, no anger, wrath or scorn
The soul anestheticised
Frozen and undone
The body a roving, singing automation.

BOB FLETCHER

A Love Dirge To The Whitehouse

(or it Soots You Right)

the cold, smoldering
savage percent are past
the scent of your stale
long unshouldered
loco pecos bags

we burn our rags
and have our own tea parties

while you wonder without blinking
(the sacks that were your eyes)
where will the ghettos get to?

to dry your hands
        will you stuff your closets
        with crumpled sheets

smeared with dirty stars
smugly
down starved throats so tightly
that the mouths won't close?

bad actors
          who can't even die
          decently.

          (a clenched hand
long before the nails
draw its own blood
will open, mark
my words)

Is it a pity
that our lack of script
must catch your off-hand dreams
with back-handed love
          (mirrors being useless even when your pants are down)
to smote the smoke from the dead-
ly innocent eyes
of feathered minds?

are we being called
(between the lines) to
          finally
          splinter your bowels
(just as your proud bombs
destroy all the rest)
or merely sear away
the rancid fatty tissue?

well fear thee well bwana
we come soon to the junction
where even your money mines
will blow up in your face
and you see, mebbe, plenty stars

where we'll have long since gotten tired
of pulling (the tattered remnants of) your coat
(patchwork—as quiet as it's kept—
of growing scars from slavebirth screaming

so
you want to take the blues
to cover your mothered oaths
and smother your confusion
in the mobile sinew
of alabama mammies?

your willing to lay down your cup and saucer
long enough to pray de lawd to strike down
Old Man River for what he done to Emmett Till
and them other boys?

well, get up
        off your goddamned knees
(no fun intended)
since you can't share the wealth
        your health cannot be gained
in some silly tactical refrain
from trembling

now please
get your double whammy uncle sammy
index finger out of my eye

can't you see that you gon' become
a statistic of your own logistics
when fedup bucks buck your brand of warpath?

for all the signs say
take heed: and do not be mislaid
as we stoke our smouldering pipes
we'll let george do it to us
no longer

so fear thee well daddio—
for, as quiet as it's kept
in all the feathered nests
the stage is unsettled
and soon we come
to bury the hatchet

NIKKI GIOVANNI

Nikki-Roasa

childhood rememberances are always a drag
if you're Black
you always remember things like living in Woodlawn
with no inside toilet
and if you become famous or something
they never talk about how happy you were to have your
                                            mother
all to yourself and
how good the water felt when you got your bath from one
                                            of those
big tubs that folk in chicago barbecue in
and somehow when you talk about home

it never gets across how much you
understood their feelings
as the whole family attended meetings about Hollydale
and even though you remember
your biographers never understand
your father's pain as he sells his stock
and another dream goes
and though you're poor it isn't poverty that
concerns you
and though they fought a lot
it isn't your father's drinking that makes any difference
but only that everybody is together and you
and your sister have happy birthdays and very good christ-
masses and I really hope no white person ever has cause to
write about me because they never understand Black love
is Black wealth and they'll probably talk about my hard
childhood and never understand that all the while I was
quite happy

CHARLES F. GORDON

The Long Night Home

i leave their fields
    a stem entangles my hair
smell a gathering of droplets—
enter the shadows yawning—
feel along tunnel walls
stretching to where we began.
the incandescent west crawls upon the roof
searches every crevice/peers intently
through a thousand eyes.
i am naked/black pollen
settles forever upon me.

journey with me, for i am weary
alone/under our wilted future
i carry to rejoin my roots...
   Look and see the strangest village.
   Death skulks among the huts
   Beaten, a slave
   Who must eat only of dead bodies.
   The living never die/the blessed are insane.
   See the tiller who files his deeds
   In straightlong rows of public eyes
   And one starves alone.
   Children make love as children will/
   Embrace the passion from whence they come
   Someday to bring forth children.
   How is it they worship the gods
   But cannot think"church?"
   The drummers play/eyes smiling distantly
   To some feeling unsymbolized
   Commanding the dancers.
the stem has fallen among their feet
drinks the moisture rolling from breast
grows stoutly toward our future...

DONALD D. GOVAN

Recollection

Mother was a wolf; snarled her long
Teeth at bad men who bothered us.
Mother went out at night when her
Friend the moon shone her the prickly
Path of thorns to find that which
Fed us.

I saw Mother weep within those eyes of
Cow, she'd look at me and my brother
And her fear would jump like a rabbit
From her eye into ours.
I looked at the dark woman and marveled
At the infinity of her eye painted with
The image of a black man from Texas; there
It was hot when he walked toward the
Sun. Wondering...Wondering...
Lonesome along her beings promonotory; she'd
Smile to her secret lover the moon.
She growled fierce when the fish face man
Smiled money. We: My brother and I thought yum
His juicy bone; but Mother wolf said we were
Human. The fish face man grew as we grew.
The larger we became the more oppressive
He is. Mother wolf wouldn't let us eat
The fish face man. We should have, but Mother
Wolf said we are human.

CAROLE GREGORY

Ghetto Lovesong—Migration

She stood hanging wash before sun
and occasionally watched the kids
gather acorns from the trees,
and when her husband came,
complaining about the tobacco spit on him,
they decided to run North
for a free evening.
She stood hanging wash in the basement
and saw the kids sneak puffs from cigarettes,

fix steel traps with cheese
and when her husband came,
complaining of the mill's drudgery,
          she burst—
said he had no hunter's heart
beat him with a broom,
became blinded by the orange sun
racing into steel mill flames
and afterwards,
sat singing   spirituals to sons.

JOHN HALL

Dark Shadows

          dark shadows
                    move into confronted
          camps
instant dismay
          to the chosen few
          —what is the
wind that produces
          such?—
                    what is the meaning
          of this omen?—
                    in structure,
this substance
          seems the
same
          unproportionate
disagreement on
          its name—
          seeds lie

wasted on
unproductive soil
          no one toils
the earth—
          barren thorns
               catch minds
     and leave them as
          evidence of
     chaotic times

ALBERT HAYNES

The Law

Oh, the tidal waves of our suffering
reach up
and shake the sky

And only those blessed with Allah's wings
escape

We have lost our gills and have long since
become obsolete
and are fleeing down
and our cries are the sounds of
wet sand against hulking metal

And our moans become like rust
scraped from metalic edges
of rusted bomb cannisters

New twisted agonies—and the gasp
as once perfect thought
form shows the limit of its whiteness

Nature rings the bell for another
cycle
(Allah, the Black Man, *this time)*

Mothers are lost and choked
their necks lay flattened, pulped.
Her sons and my brothers argue
and fight each other only to anger the tide.

Oh, the beauty of that anger
as it is building and rising
straining liquid fingers
stroking heavyweight clouds
pulling them down, those forces in the sky.

John Coltrane—Come back
don't play and run away
Your dream rehearsal we must all attend.

Atop there—those fingers of liquid
Black fingers, chirping angels—soul directors
while gods of war ride along the top
of giant tidal waves rehearse the places
they will take when sadness bearers
desperately imitate fish complete with
gills and scales
The seventh veil-angels painted with Black copper emerge

The gate there yonder
made for by dark legs
and horn shaped mouths
giant god heads upon sandstone bodies
being lowered awesomely near the gate—our efforts
antlike in the sand

The new world——hold your thoughts
The new world——the eyes remain open
The new world——Magic gravity holds him to a chair
                    at water's edge
                    sitting like the giant shell, as the torrent
                    and shaking, moves through his senses
                    He desperately maintains his blackness
                    un-emptying, like a sponge

                    While the rest of us are beaten
                    into pebbles, plowshares, and fossils.

DAVID HENDERSON

Psychedelic Firemen

psychedelic firemen
all over america
                New York City/Babylon
everyone high
                meat of animals
                tropical sugars
                LSD crime
america is a land of drug addicts
ones who have blown their minds
historically locking-up the mellow

        crime in the streets
                a slogan

walk his city by sundown
witness
flames upon roof tops

along the piers
palisades crumbling spires
organized amusement parks/fright-death
upon roller-coasters with one end   only
passengers fallout backwards
into mad carnival music of the streets
sirens imported from druid regions of europe
world wide police believe them
the weirdest
roller coaster through manhattan by underground express
iron cars trains of auschwitz
jangling metal grit   subway air

MAN DOES NOT BELONG UNDERGROUND
yet the blue men
of the eerie druid regions
patrol in place of dogs mad
metal iron symphony   insanity
to dope-heads no matter
strobe-beam police cars swirling at subway entrance
"oh my god, not another subway crime!"
underground housewives scream in despair
women waiting to be raped by the "A" train
fast metal shaft
black native express
sweatdripping cars drooping ubangi lips/waiting for the haul
from midtown 59th
to harlem 125th
sixty-six blocks
of pillage/ shreiking white women of washington heights
mass rape of ornette
the trumpet boy
GENERAL MOTORS WORLD'S FAIR ATTENDANCE
TOPS VATICAN PAVILION

AMERICA!
    is a land of speeding cars
        drapes the moon
phosphorous   fart fire burns   carbohydrates
racist sugar   napalm-whiskey

speeding cars
lights white green flicker
        white lightening
          along highways & underground tubes
huge poster signs
        wood posters billboard platters   neon
          phallic & decaying

red devil paint/ alcoholic white light
upon flourescence
        verses sky
        king blue
PLASTER WALLS DON'T BURN
          they say
firemen flashing from posters
reeling from billboards
clutching little girls
moby dick his eyes
mommy her mouth
        fireman leers
I HAVE SAVED THIS LITTLE GIRL IN NAME OF THE
                            STATE

KEEP NEW YORK PLASTERED
face of fire
methedrine skin erosion pop
flashing white crystals
        lining streets/ white Xmas
blaze   out   strobe beam   swing   black   light

camera weird focus
   intrepid fireman
     hands up little girls dress
fireman reels
intrepid child does not scream
collapsing walls
sirens high dog howl/ end of a mother's scream prolonged
      in the hearts of our countrymen
   door burst flailing axes
swords saxophones
broken back furniture smoke fire wood

    WHILE
   thru harlem fire rages water cycles
    weekends of fun/ partying/ burning flesh
    this thanksgiving
  for the natives who hunt for the feast
  but do not partake/
     silent natives screaming
     thru western guns swords axes
     tall tenor saxophones
  blaring black trumpets/ page of swords
     spanish habana
 African chants/ long-legged dance
to the bullfight
     stab the beast
    don't waste a stroke by spear
   symbolic death for your meat/
   harlem raging
    trumpet tenor axes blare
   MIDNIGHT HOUR
    /sugar shards high music
   to tumult of psychedelic
  artillery
     of cities insane/

CALVIN C. HERNTON

Elements Of Grammar

to little john

1

There are no stars which fell on Alabama,
Georgia, Mississippi, New York. There never
Were. The Lucky Dime Salon is around

The corner from the Brooklyn Navy Yard.
Stevedores, seamen. truck drivers, cock roaches,
Construction workers,
And other rough faced villains
Drink liquor and beer and tell a lot of

Lies and a lot of trues
About all the different kind of
Women they done
Made love to.
With his testicles and penis and muscles
And elephant's hide
That fit slack in the joints

Man is a lonely animal.

2

Around the corner from the Brooklyn Navy Yard
This is the way the world is.
If I were the woman who walked with the gods
I would know that long before Bismarck
The black Tribes came over from

Africa and made havoc with Constantinople
Sent the white-robed landlords running for their
Lives into the Mediterranean—
If I were woman who gave birth to God
I would stretch my thighs

And give Alabama, Georgia, Mississippi
And New York
Some good pussy.

In the Lucky Dime below the deck
There is a jewelled throne
Around which the sea is served in
Formaldehyde hallucinations.

3

No stars fell on Alabama. None but
The dead living know the horror of Georgia,
Mississippi and New York.

At night where stars fall, you can
Hear the mourning and the groaning—at night
By the godgold of the moon
You can see the blood of the scarecrow
Bleeding on the deck below:

It was early one morning
I was on my way to school
That was the morning I broke my
Mother's rule.

WASN'T IT SAD WHEN THE GREAT TITANIC WENT DOWN

Sin and salvation
Seven comes eleven
This is the way the world is.

4

Around the corner from the Lucky Dime
Salon
In the yard of the Brooklyn Navy
There is much semen on the ground
And punctured prophylactics decaying
In the summer heat.

I give you the Statue of Liberty
George Washington Monument
And the Fastest Train Out Of Town!
All crows cock when the owl is blind—
A bullet in the night
A bomb, a knee in the groin,
And a red neck cracker

Pounding his thick muddy boots
Down on the belly of a black woman
Sprawled in the Mississippi gravel
Beneath a signboard advertising sun lotion
For the obscenity

Of America.
With his little wee wee tucked under
The folds of his flabby belly
And trousers bagging his rump
Screaming and raving about the purity
Of the white race,
I give you the cock roach of civilization!

Man is a lonely animal.

So we mill around down here in the Lucky Dime—
Construction worker, truck driver, stevedore...
REMEMBER
THAT SHIP TITANIC WHITE FOLKS BUILT LONG
                                    TIME AGO
SO BIG AND HIGHCLASS IT COULD NOT SINK
AND THEY LET ONE NEGRO WORK ON THERE
                                    JANITOR
AND THEN THE SHIP SUNK MYSTERIOUSLY AND
                                    THE NEGRO
JUMPED OFF AND STARTED SWIMMING THE WHOLE
                                    WIDE OCEAN
HIS NAME WAS "SHINE"...

Up from the deck jumped the Captain's daughter
Screaming! *Shine! Shine! Save poor me*
I'll give you all the white loving a black scarecrow
Like you need!
Hallucinations

Of Georgia, Mississippi, Alabama, Florida,
Detroit, Chicago, New York, Boston, Tennessee,
New Jersey, Louisiana,
This is the way the world is.

Wasn't it sad!
An iceberg
A bullet
The moaning and the groaning--
        at night
        by the silver of the stars.

QUENTIN HILL

Time Poem

It's time   for bloody WAtusis to romp through the streets
wielding spears like burning crosses
automatic spears   500 rounds a minute   infrared spears
spears that knock out tanks
spears that deliver warheads   spears that destroy
                                                    powerplants
and how to do it
go to the precinct   say hello to the sargeant
put your spear between his eyes and pull the trigger
for those bullshit teachers who lied and gave you a hard
                                                    time
eternalrecess   take them off
death to cracker and his toys
and that which went down before
        artifacts of lost culture: cigar store Indians
Jean Crain and Roy Wilkins
        ghosts walking along KNEEGRO tarbaby streets
orange pants and beaver hats
restless   waiting to impale the moon
oppressive foot treading water and azure sky
to drown   in libraries
dangerous books enter   blind fingers grope and stay there
red flows violently from the bullet holes   and
from between the legs of dead books
        the leaves of paper bring forth dead children—
at the high school
        cracker tries to subtley mash our skulls
we resist and are forced to leave at gunpoint
in the street

    the cops curse us   divide us   kill us
beat us with the invisible rubber hose
some die
they are buried or become crackers
we   turn to smoke and wine   maybe stronger stuff
we try to drown each others pain by going down for bubble
                                                      gum
yet some nights tears still well up in our eyes   or
we break our fists hitting thick heads
now that some of us realize what must be done
DO IT
and here is how it may be

     Scene 1: A deserted city street; large buildings surround-
ing a plaza. The plaza is constructed of granite blocks. Each
block has an inscription. Closer inspection gives an under-
standing of what it all means. Blocks on the right center
read: The Soul Survivors—thought that their ears would
bring them lasting fame & fortune—each died of cancer of
the throat. Chet Baker—convicted of lick stealing cause of
death unknown. Hugh Addonizio former mayor of Newark—
convicted of trying to enslave the major portion of his city's
population   executed.

     Scene 2: White. Snow and ice everywhere implies
someplace like the North Pole or Antarctica. In the side of
a mountain of snow, an indentation, call it cave, can be
seen. At the mouth of the cave is a sign: COWS— Congress
On Whiteys Survival; inside two hundred white people hold
their annual convention.

EVERETT HOAGLAND

Night Interpreted

the shredded sunset,
jagged bleeding hymen of night taken
and preferring
the empathetic night
breathing hot on me the greeneyed panther
summer night
blending black
distantly with the simmering solid night
asphalt
the blind mute night
compassionate
reveals no circling vultures
contain me
warm womb night!
night skinned woman
hold me in the night air velvet
of your light night arms
night
the shadow of tomorrow or
the shroud of
dead days
dawn the orifice of hours
futilly invites me
i
a minor darkness
living in absolute night
yet
not sleeping and fearing dreams

ELTON HILL-ABU ISHAK

Theme Brown Girl

for gloria

I have watched you dancing
in the streets   of Dakar
                    robed in soft darkness;
bending over steel-edged counters
                                        in Detroit
face slick & hot with kitchen-sweat.

I have known your brown lips
in the sullen Congo
when your world was black,
        How beautiful you were there
        breasted with Africa,
But your new world is white
and you are mistress in another's house;

And when they called you "Nigger"
        were you not afraid?
And did the spit & whips & clubs
        & scars of hatred
a nation heaved on your head,
did they edge your beauty

I have watched you
                                in Haiti
crowned with bandanna & bathing in coolness
and in Harlem
                    lonely on midnight corners;

and in Watts
             swollen with the sickness
of slums and poverty.
Yet,
          I still see Africa in your eyes
          girl with the spirit of a leopard
          tell the world that time
          will never mark your face.

LANCE JEFFERS

My Blackness Is The Beauty Of This Land

My blackness is the beauty of this land,
my blackness,
tender and strong, wounded and wise,
my blackness:
I, drawling black grandmother, smile muscular and sweet,
unstraightened white hair soon to grow in earth,
work thickened hand thoughtful and gentle on grandson's head,
my heart is bloody-razored by a million memories' thrall:

          remembering the crook-necked cracker who spat
               on my naked body,
          remembering the splintering of my son's spirit
               because he remembered to be proud
          remembering the tragic eyes in my daughter's
               dark face when she learned her color's
               meaning,

and my own dark rage a rusty knife with teeth to gnaw
          my bowels,

my agony ripped loose by anguished shouts in Sunday's
          humble church,
my agony rainbowed to ecstasy when my feet oversoared
          Montgomery's slime,

ah, this hurt, this hate, this ecstasy before I die,
and all my love a strong cathedral!
My blackness is the beauty of this land!

Lay this against my whiteness, this land!
Lay me, young Brutus stamping hard on the cat's tail,
gutting the Indian, gouging the nigger,
booting Little Rock's Minniejean Brown in the buttocks and
                                        boast,
          my sharp white teeth derision-bared as I the conqueror
               crush!
Skyscraper-I, white hands burying God's human clouds
                                        beneath
          the dust!
Skyscraper-I, slim blond young Empire
          thrusting up my loveless bayonet to rape the sky,
then shrink all my long body with filth and in the gutter lie
as lie I will to perfume this armpit garbage,

While I here standing black beside
wrench tears from which the lies would suck the salt
to make me more American than America...
But yet my love and yet my hate shall civilize this land,
this land's salvation.

ALICIA LEY JOHNSON

Black Lotus/ a prayer

I

eternal spirit
of dead dried
autumn leaves
never seen in
B-L-A-C-K G-H-E-T-T-O-S
of this morbid country
let
a human
polyploid
triple in number
inside
the
ooctid
&
spermatid of
black beings/
to produce
powerful
causes for
candid
creatures.
come——
come——a
way with
your imbecilic ideas
of not being able

to CEASE your killing
of INNOCENT SOULS––
                    the LOTUS
                    will rise/ beyond stem
                    & root/ to an unknown shoot
                    that exists in the heaven of
                    LOTUS LAND.

                II

the blue african lotus
will taste
sweet to
black thick lips
&
foul to white
sour serpent lips.
W-E/ W-I-L
K-I-L
your beauty &
squeeze your
warts & varicose veins
from your old women's legs
W-E/ W-I-L
send messages
of death to your
children
swimming in
south/ american pools.
W-E/ W-I-L
take your oil refineries
& distileries & soak
your own bodies
til-they become

[75]

sliperi with oil buds
bouncing all over
them.

III

BLACK LOTUS of
ghana
rhodesia
south west africa
of
vietnam
china
cuba
and the AMERICAS/ feed
your bellies with
cultural chocolates
shout hosannas of holiness
raise your voice
     bring autumn leaves
     to the ghettos/
               let the fruit
               of the
               LOTUS
               perform on the
               USURPERS in
OUR ghettos
they'll forget
and become
dreamy
& WE WIL
then make
our move.

    a-men

HOWARD JONES

Fall T O

Man rejects imprisonment
Seeking perfection
                    in art...
Accepting, forgiving, just giving
Frailties, crimes—we will not
save
        AMERICAN CHARITY
IS AN EXTRA BOOK OF
MATCHES
            the masked attempt
                to elude contempt:
                    contrived speech
The spark of your leaving   is a leech.
        being loved in me
        is fanned by what wind would be
        (but a breeze)
        to set ablaze the dull dry
        leaves of scented mentalities—

POLISH YOUR FAILURES WELL AND GUESTS WILL
   PRAISE YOUR TASTE IN MODERN FURNITURE

        As in some dark and quivering moment
            in glaringly lit loneliness
            where night comes on
            as a strengthened drought
            and freedom wars on idle thoughts
the depths of me cry aloud
THE GRAVE IS DIGGING UNEARTHED SOIL
IN WHICH THE COCOON IS TO BE SPUN

FOR THE RAISING OF THE SEED
TRIES WAITING EXALTATION.

LEROI JONES

W.W.

Back home the black women are all beautiful,
and the white ones fall back, cutoff from 1000
years stacked booty, and Charles of The Ritz
where jooshladies turn into billy burke in
       blueglass
kicks. With wings, and jingly-bew-teeful things.
The black women in Newark are fine. Even with
all that grease in their heads. I mean even
the ones where the wigs a
slide around, and they coming at you 75 degrees
       off course.
I could talk to them. Bring them around.
To something.
Some kind of quick course, on the sidewalk,
       like Hey baby,
why don't you take that thing off yo' haid.
You look like
Miss Muffett in a runaway ugly machine.
I mean. Like that.

NORMAN JORDAN

Feeding The Lions

They come into
our neighborhood
with the sun
an army of
social workers

carrying briefcases
filled with lies
and stupid grins
Passing out relief
checks
and food stamps
hustling from one
apartment to another
so they can fill
their quota
and get back out
before dark.

BOB KAUFMAN

I, Too, Know What I Am Not

No, I am not death wishes of sacred rapists, singing
      on candy gallows.
No, I am not spoor of Creole murderers hiding
      in crepe-paper bayous.
No, I am not yells of some assassinated inventor, locked
      in his burning machine.
No, I am not forced breathing of Cairo's senile burglar,
      in lead shoes
No, I am not Indian-summer fruit of Negro piano tuners,
      with muslin gloves.
No, I am not noise of two-gun senators, in hallowed
      peppermint hall.
No, I am not pipe-smoke hopes of cynical chiropractors,
      traffickers in illegal bone.
No, I am not pitchblende curse of Indian suicides,
      in bonnets of flaming water.

No, I am not soap-powder sighs of impotent window washers,
　　　in pants of air.
No, I am not kisses of tubercular sun addicts, smiling
　　　through rayon lips.
No, I am not chipped philosopher's tattered ideas sunk
　　　in his granite brain.
No, I am not cry of amethyst heron, winged stone in flight
　　　from cambric bullets.
No, I am not sting of the neurotic bee, frustrated
　　　in cheesecloth gardens.
No, I am not peal of muted bell, clapperless
　　　in the faded glory.
No, I am not report of silenced guns, helpless
　　　in the pacifist hands.
No, I am not call of wounded hunter, alone
　　　in the forest of bone.
No, I am not eyes of the infant owls hatching
　　　the roofless night.
No, I am not the whistle of Havana whores with cribs
　　　of Cuban death.
No, I am not shriek of Bantu children, bent
　　　under pennywhistle whips.
No, I am not whisper of the African trees,
　　　leafy Congo telephones.
No, I am not Leadbelly of blues, escaped from guitar jails.
No, I am not anything that is anything I am not.

ETHRIDGE KNIGHT

He Sees Through Stone

He sees through stone
he has the secret
eyes this old black one
who sits under prison skies

sits pressed by the sun
against the western wall
his pipe between purple gums

the years fall
like over-ripe plums
bursting red flesh
on the dark earth

his time is not my time
but I have known him
In a time now gone

he led me trembling cold
into the dark forest
taught me the secret rites
to take a woman
to be true to my brothers
to make my spear drink
the blood
of my enemies

now black cats circle him
flash white teeth
snarl at the air
mashing green grass beneath
shining muscles
ears peeling his words
he smiles
he knows

the hunt   the enemy
he has the secret eyes
he sees through stone

DON L. LEE

Re-Act For Action

for brother H. Rap Brown

re-act to animals:
>   cage them in zoos.
re-act to inhumanism:
>   make them human.
re-act to nigger toms:
>   with spiritual acts of love & forgiveness
>   or with real acts of force.
re-act to yr/self:
>   or are u too busy tryen to be cool
>   like tony curtis & twiggy?
re-act to whi-te actors:
>   understand their actions:
>   faggot actions & actions against yr/dreams
re-act to yr/brothers & sisters:
>   love.
re-act to whi-te actions:
>   with real acts of blk/action.
>   BAM BAM BAM

re-act to act against actors
who act out pig-actions against
your acts & actions that keep
you re-acting against their acts & actions
stop.
act in a way that will cause them
to act the way you want them to act
in accordance with yr/acts & actions:
>   human acts for human beings

re-act
NOW niggers
& you won't have to
act
false-actions
at
your/children's graves.

CY LESLIE

On Riots

Incentive
born in ancient
drum
        battles
obscene values,
archaic faiths.

Exploited blacks
stand grounded
in strong
        belief;
And now must
        wreck
the diabolic clock
        of moderation.

WORTH LONG

Arson And Cold Lace

(or how i yearn to Burn Baby Burn)

We have found you out
False faced America
We have found you out
We have found you out
False farmers
We have found you out
The sparks of suspicion
Are melting your waters
and water can't drown them
These fires a-burning
and firemen can't calm them
With falsely appeasing
and preachers can't pray
With hopes for deceiving
Nor leaders deliver
A lecture on losing
Nor teachers inform them
The chosen are choosing
For now is the fire
and fires won't answer
To logic and listening
and hopefully seeming
Hot flames must devour
The kneeling and fleeing
and torture the masters
Whose idiot pleading
Gits lost in the echoes
Of dancing and bleeding

We have found you out
False farmers
We have found you out
We have found you out
False faced America
We have found you out

AUDRE LORDE

What My Child Learns Of The Sea

What my child learns of the sea
Of the summer thunder
Of the bewildering riddle that hides at the vortex of spring
She will learn in my twilight
And childlike
Revise every autumn.

What my child learns
As her winters fall out of time
Ripened in my own body
To enter her eyes with first light.

This is why
More than blood,
Or the milk I have given
One day a strange girl will step
To the back of a mirror
Cutting my ropes
Of sea and thunder and sun.
Of the way she will taste her autumns
Toast-brittle, or warmer than sleep
And the words she will use for winter
I stand already condemned.

CLARENCE MAJOR

Down Wind Against The Highest Peaks

you dig instant   revolution: against
rotten meat. Nauseous mariners Black
spirits, disobedient ancient sailors,
the ship of our lineal

navy, in white fog. The odor of   death:
they try to force us to eat, live on the
garbage flesh, the thick worms
wiggling in the trick whipped on us: like

I saw   these Russian dudes of 1917 in this
Stanislavski film, with the same bullshit
for cats who simply had to take over
and cut those fuckfaces up into little pieces, a

view unexpected, and drop   them into
the psychic black waters of Albert Ryder.
As now: these viscious concrete tides of police
riot the soft, brilliant   dark-

ness of our natural! conflict
of self & state, while my ancient brains/ eyes
cruise the gulf of our history, taste
the salt of our future in their eye

measured by the dust: now   on our war-
ships tall narcotic structures moving
along 63rd St. as across the atlantic trade, a
disposition of vain navigated greed

or was it a water-
fountain, *all white*   in Texas, in Georgia, my
neck   turning concrete, "Stop nigger
these bricks, stop in midair

or my corrosion increasing as I pass their
sunglass-covered whiteeyes in Mexico, these
institutions against the dark mysticism of
us. I go down   wind, against the highest

peaks of my acknowledgement of their
tired, decaying strength. Technology moves in.
Measured into dust, the return of Africa
the destruction

the use of Tonto Sambo Willie & almost any
moment in my passage, the time-table
of my essence, is a reference.
The super-blonde has even invaded the billboards
of Mexico: an asskissing nation. Behind my
memories the trip of junkies of 39th St.
who one day become tour-guides of
their mental sea-

sickness. Armed spirits,
chasing Rudolph Valentino. His ass complete-
ly
out of the desert: where he drops off

the edge of the world, a
nervous-wreck.
Which ain't revolutionary, you
dig?

JOSEPH MAJOR

Poem For Thel–The Very Tops Of Trees

...and two bird-children
harmonized
far inside a yellow field..
knitting a patchwork
nest of dawn-grey
madrigals..
weighing each straw to
make certain it was encrusted
with golden right memories,
inhaling every amber minute
as an adventure into
wonderland
        merrily terrily wispy purples
        singing gayly out of breath yes
        through swinging high-wire carnival's
        trapeze one, two, children buckle my shoe

...and when escorting high
the wind into the sky..
dancing magicly through
a thousand seasons..
building shrines on
lyrical wingtips..
they were free–free smiling
..and when, if ever it's
time for them to go,
they'll return to earth
only after a muted trumpet's
exhale of candle-bright odes
has taught them that they

[88]

have only to journey into
the others eyes to find
anywhere they want

merrily terrily wispy purples
singing gayly out of breath yes
through swinging high-wire carnival's
trapeze one, two, children buckle my shoe

...and the air will be
song, verse and love
I wish you
as I would wish you
a wreath of
green-green melodies.

JUNE MEYER

All The World Moved

All the world moved next to me strange
I grew on my knees
in hats and taffets trusting
the holy water to run
like grief from a brownstone
cradling.

Blessing a fear of the anywhere
face too pale to be family
my eyes wore ribbons
for Christ on the subway
as weekly as holiness
in Harlem.

God knew no East no West no South
no Skin nothing I learned like
traditions of sin but later
life began and strangely
I survived His innocence
without my own.

ERNIE MKALIMOTO

Energy For A New Thang

(e equals blackness squared)

the curious twists
and bent turns of pain
pretzel spirits unwinding un
ravelling babbling screaming
stumbling to embrace
the infinite petaled dawn of
spring blackness
cloud spheres shimmering behind
the trees of floating silver gases
purple seahorses with over
ripe penises galloping boogity
boogity across the waves of orange sea
beds and speckled algae-green lace a
dead owl blinks blind yellow

fire
in the spirit in the
hands in the eyes in the
brain in the thighs in the
sex of the rising panther

for ever let us pro
create these radiant suns and
sons of suns with brown sugarscoops
of energy sucked from all the tongueless
tasty corners of black unfulfilled dreams
expressions
expressions
of invisible laser chants pul sing
from andrew hill's steel fingers/ guaran
teed to set us back on our souls again

JOSEPH M. MOSLEY JR.

Black Church On Sunday

Exiled
    from places of honor about the Throne of Grace
in Saint Mary's Cathedral
These overdressed Black men, women and children
hold fast the Faith—not of *their* Fathers—
returning now from Religion's Baptist sing-song
in the rickety storefront Church all peeling paint
and creaking plaster, down the street from the
Liquor Store across from the Homosexual Bar.
Exiles
    from polished Pine pews and Redwood kneelers
they attend the God of Abraham—not Christ Jesus—
though they bathe in His Name.
More kin than kind to Hebrew Pawnbrokers and
    Candy Store merchants on the streets of the world.
Now wrapped from weekday wrongs and run-over shoes
    they go, encased in fine linens which startle their
Black bodies to a strange new stiffness, their Black
faces still reflecting Light from communion with
the Unknown God.

Percy/ 68

I got a friend named Percy
Who Booga-loo's down to
A fine finish
    Just like the Coca Cola
    People on the bathroom
    Wall;
He walks a sweating broad home
Every night,
A newspaper Idol of Annie Oakley
Trying to learn how to shoot straight.
    He dances in the temples of the wolf like
A little-biddy nigger doll with big powers
In congress.
    Oh...Percy! the people say. Git it! they
    Say. Work it! they say.
    And all the time he say...
"Just like Daniel Boone, coming back to
Work these bears."

LARRY NEAL

Orishas

Is the eternal voice, Coltrane is.
is black people slowly moving,
harlem faces slow dance in the blue night air,
is black people moving against the drum pressing hearts.
run that down to them, those there standing
on the corners: let it roll—let it roll.
come to us again, there is no peace here;

the sound weaves, tearing slowly beating hearts,
substance of energy-death, and eternal rebirth
make us a pure thing, a pure black singing thing
in the voices jarring the night sounds;
against this rumor pale things fall dead
scurry like rats for the sewer caves
Great voice in me sing, be me, be my essence
great Shango, press into us, we are
children before you; or at best shadows of ourselves,
fleshless movements in the funky hallways,
rubbed up against her, macking on the living room floor,
pressed for time. hurry, hurry, momma be home soon,
kiss wetly, and smell the body, kiss quickly. touch.
leave yourself with me baby, leave yourself in the mirror,
in the dishes scrapped, ready for washing.

Commemoration

Who are the dead?
who are the long list of names in the oceans
who are the figures standing in the cabin doors
as the train highballs North
Who are the wailing children,
bodies ripped into bits of flesh?
I catch aspects of their profiles,
am wound around them like a serpent
grasping for life.
whose eyes are these, gouged out
mucus smeared in the red earth,
figure hanging tarred above the lynch fire?
what bodies are these crushed and maimed,
or brains kicked out on the piss pavements
of the cities?
How many aspects of truth do you need Negro leaders?
How many angles are there to any story?
Whose church was that now charred smoldering in time?

Whose mamma getting laid in the cotton patch;
whose orishas call blood-warnings?
Whose shall die, and die, and die, and die?
Whose soul fucked on the assembly floor?
whose mind picked clean in air-conditioned offices?
whose children shot to pieces in newark tenements?
whose blood is that efficient lackey-tom motherfuckers?

MICHAEL NICHOLAS

Today: The Idea Market

Today, I will see some empty spaces
Of people and how they go along,
As tin foil and nerves blend
Into more people as they follow along...
Today, Cyclops bellows from tv tape
The same re-heard sounds of violence.
I have a candy-apple red B-52.
I'm napalm in Watts.
I shall be gas from other hydrogens.
Today, I must go to Biology class
To give this murdered frog to my Professor.
Today, Pushkin will bleed in ancient snow.
Today, my unborn son will grow to war.
Today, I will use my anti-knowledge
To understand the images of pine rope,
That pulls beneath my outer skull.
Today, I will toss more periods and colons
Onto a page that cannot understand why
There is more of the same,
Especially,
Today...

DT OGILVIE

Last Letter To The Western Civilization

"what a waste of a beautiful girl!'"?!
oh, my God,
what a waste of a beautiful
PEOPLE
you pretend to understand
you sympathize
you express concern
hiding
    behind sugar-plum visions
       of eternal
          life
so afraid
    to face reality
that's right, baby, reality, DEATH
    yeah, yuh know
    you, baby, YOU!! are going to
        D...I...E
hah, hah
yellow-minded, weak-livered, simple cowards
afraid to face the simple fact that
        life ends,
it ends baby, dig it. IT ENDS.
repeating some incredible off-the-wall bullshit
about
    "yeah, well, uh, i want to do what i can, but, uh,
    well, i know that it's not really *that* important
    to me; i can't spend my whole life worrying
    about it"
HYPOCRITE
you delude yourselves

[95]

with honeyed dreams of
        longevity
you write theses and manifestos on
        the sanctity of life
you riddle your brains with
        the holey sacredness of life
yet, *every day* of your lives,
        of *each* of your lives
you
murder another individual
HYPOCRITE
preaching the humanity of man
eulogizing on the equality of man
you mothering hypocrite
i feel sorry for you
as i would pity a cripple or a blind man
i pity you
for you are crippled of human-ness
                        human essence
                        human emotion
for you are blind to the self-induced ravages
        of your weltanschauung
for you cannot see that, in the end, through your
        own bent to self-destruction,
your own efforts to self-annihilation will be
        rewarded
yes, i know why you have these propensities to genocide,
        these suicidal tendencies
for
had i perpetrated
        and perpetuated
the same egregious crimes against, in reality,
        myself
that you had

had i committed these horrors
      even in dreams
i would kill myself
realizing
that dreams are the seeds of reality
yes, your death-wish will be answered
for
      being imperfect men
      you made an imperfect work:
      that of the imperfectly brainwashed black man
you programmed our minds to be bleached
but,
      in your natural
            stupidity
you left a corner untouched
   and
         it
               was
                     enough
            to
      lead
   us
to
dye our minds back to black
the dark color
      composed of
      many colors
      many shades
of humanistic tendencies
of human-ness
of human
      beings
who reject being
bleached of humanity

and emotion
and good will
and self-respect
and self-confidence
you tried to tear the fabric of our US-ness
but you left enough for us to mend ourselves
and to make our selves stronger
than before
and you realize
in the depths
of your
soulessness
that we shall conquer
without a doubt!

CHARLES PATTERSON

Listen

Hear the sound
It is un-like any other
The ears are in constant pain
From the sound
Of Blood dripping from a wound
Centuries long
Each drop that falls crashes into time
Quickly drys and waits for another drop of agony
Descending like war bombs
Composed of destruction
Listen with one ear for the sound
Cover both—you are there
Living the sound
Hear the Blood ooze from the wound

Falling through time
On ears which are deaf to transition
Stop listen to the sound
It is un-like any other
Touch it squeeze it between space
Now attempt to wash it off
Fingers which are bleeding into time
Cup the sound, imprison it.
Then open time's doors and let loose
Your misery and awaken deaf mute men

RAY PATTERSON

You Are The Brave

You are the brave who do not break
In the grip of the mob when the blow comes straight
To the shattered bone; when the sockets shriek;
When your arms lie twisted under your back.

Good men holding their courage slack
In their frightened pockets see how weak
The work that is done; and feel the weight
Of your blood on the ground for their spirit's sake;

And build their anger, stone on stone;
Each silently, but not alone.

TOM POOLE

I

wonder why
some

people
leave the
front

porch
light still
on

in
the burning
bright

hotness
of summer
day

noontime.

N. H. PRITCHARD

Metagnomy

Amid the non-committed compounds of the mind
an imageless gleaming
weather haunts as yet unknown
and taunts through a chemistry of ought

that changes
courses
seemingly
as if a bird in flight
a word
forgotten
in the wind's wont

What aim counsels such again
unto the sylvan down of wombs
what never ever stand
causes such manifest stasis
to ride only upon that movement the earth provides

Often the setting mind
like dusk ajourns
as though the knowing
as though the glowing

To seek
to find
a lance
to pierce the possible

Often a wish defined
like lust returns
as though upon an alter
blood is broken
as meat
is rite
and accuring pagan
crucifixion

Enchantments abound about the abysses of a mind
often blinded by the cataracts of curt concern
while aim sits dauntlessly on a pedestal
being pecked upon
by the wind's wont

HELEN QUIGLESS

Concert

This garden too pleasant
the moon too near pools
of water avoid

>   reflecting smooth sketches
>   of "Spain" in man's desires.

How now brown drummer?
as you hold him in your
spell
>   that man of sax.
>   That princely black
>   dreams aloud the
>   agony of his race

>   as his lips grip
>   the telescopic view
>   which curves abruptly
>   and stares upon their face.

Sailing through the air,
a taloned-shriek
draws blood from the ears.

And long the cry rings

    against stone museum walls
    against city sounds
    against the dying sun's light
    against spiral statues oblivious of rain
    against lily pads and fish of gold
    against minds that concentrate
    against love that tolerates
    against the multitude

     pale

          so

               that

                    smiles

   fade
   from triumphant sounds of music.

Rings cry the long until
it shudders and dies,

and sweetness comes to him.

DUDLEY RANDALL

Blackberry Sweet

Black girl black girl
lips as curved as cherries
full as grape bunches
sweet as blackberries

Black girl black girl
when you walk you are

magic as a rising bird
or a falling star

Black girl black girl
what's your spell to make
the heart in my breast
jump   stop   shake

LENNOX RAPHAEL

Infants Of Summer

Infants of summer, how weak you are these springs
How high your color shows when smiles protrude. But
Are you really there. In this strange land. Where
The flesh is weak in style. Your leaves are falling
And this wind called change is blowing in your eyes
Are you falling from this wind? It's hard to tell
When people die so neat. It's hard to tell
When pain becomes so very very hard
To tell when wars are thought. Not fought as love
Can bite the flesh and hang upon the blood. A
Servile pain. Or anything that makes out to be several gods
At once. Not caring how to firm their smiles in dust.
Infants of summer, how weak you are these springs
How much it seems nothing changes. Matters not how. Or
                                                much
Without the sanction of blood for every cup
To overflowing. Til the heart is dunked. And made whole
In going where even the seasons must obey the calender
Of events spaced out in our lives as a manicured saloon
Of graves propped out of their lonely inhabitants who
Even at that stage. Must search a reason for their fate
Much as we search now for ourselves in a fogbank of hope

AMIR RASHIDD

Eclipse

The blue smoke eclipsed
a red light
That illuminates
The cubical in which
I have become prisoner
Awaiting trial
For some misunderstood
Crime against the state.

The rebellious figures
Disorder themselves in
The center of the well,
The voices in the other
World crying to me:
"Come," they said, "get it now.
Death is cheap. Death is cheap."

Yes, death is cheap.
This is the sound
Yhsy tsnh in my ears like
The mourning wails at Satan's funeral.
The boisterous sound rang
Through the market place
Undeterred in the ears of
The wiser ones who fled.

The counters were lined
With the empty markers
For the vanished grains

Of black clay that
Cobble the road to Manana.

The gutters are filled
With the swollen bodies
Of those unable to see their day
Further in a cell, trapped,
Their heads popping above
The seal breaking the
Sun rushing through the window!

I escaped into the dark
Day only to become
Weary after running
Through the narrow streets,
Crawling by the dead,
Who lay beheaded
In the dormitory of leeches.

I stood facing their pale
And morbid executioner,
Peering down into his vacant eyes
As he drank rum stolen from
The tenders of the fire.
He danced with a frozen corpse.
I touched her hand and she
                    disintegrated.

Warriors Prancing, Women Dancing...

Warriors prancing, women dancing, while children
sang their praise. Evening suns blaze we at pre-
sent infant aged men and women life we laid. from
the grass huts through our loins poured warriors
prancing, women too were made.

In our big black Africa, behind the nature thick
Mana and God.
No lies, no tricks, supported by shady alibis.

Then o' a mighty sea did we slave side by side
manipulated, masqueraded God's creation til we
seek refuge in our shadows.

Now warriors prancing, dancing, singing of their
own praise. Lost in a lie while the spirits still
beat a warrior's drums. Thumbing, pumbing out a
truth freedom and God shall overcome.
Waving hair, waving minds, wondering when will he
come. Naturals shining, glorifying trying to bring
back warriors to the evening suns.

Running over plains, and jungle. king of truth and
beast. Womens' shadows reflecting lies from neon
streets of hell and death, not dancing by a freaked
beast's noose. Sons pure, black as truth, not won-
dering through a haze of helplessness of definite
disaster, shamed by their fathers, hating their mothers,
loving the beastly devil who murders us. killing their
brothers, selling their sisters and their souls for a

devils purse filled only with misery, debt, pain and
death.

Warriors fighting, dynamiting hell's walls, U.S.A.
Breaking chains, changing names, hundlallah humdlahhah
this is freedom's way. Babies cryin' fathers dying,
kill this awful place, evenings in a three day riot
mothers bore black sons to reinforce the black brigade
at the lenox ave. front.

God is alive, christ was born again in a basement apart-
ment B 1. First is first last is death truth is God is
first and
freedom.

EUGENE REDMOND

Gods In Vietnam

Mechanical
Oracles dot the sky,
Casting shadows on the sun.
Instead of manna
Leaflets fall
To resurrect the coals
Dead from the week's bombing.

Below
In the jungle,
Flaming alters
Buckle under prophecies;
And smoke whimpers
In the west wind.

Dry seas hide the
Cringing fold
While fishermen leap from clouds,
Nets blooming
On their lean bodies.

The sun slumps,
Full;
Before it sleeps
Solemn chaplains come,
Their voices choked
In suspicious silence.

ISHMAEL REED

I Am A Cowboy In The Boat Of Ra

> *"The devil must be forced to reveal any such
> physical evil (potions, charms, fetishes, etc.)
> still outside the body and these must be
> burned."* —Rituale Romanum, *published
> 1947, endorsed by the coat of arms and
> introduction letter from Francis Cardinal
> Spellman*

I am a cowboy in the boat of Ra,
sidewinders in the saloons of fools
bit my forehead   like   O
the untrustworthiness of Egyptologists
who do not know their trips. Who was that
dog-faced man? they asked, the day I rode
from town.

School marms with halitosis cannot see
the Nefertiti fake chipped on the run by slick
germans, the hawk behind Sonny Rollins' head or
the ritual beard of his axe; a longhorn winding
its bells thru the Field of Reeds.

I am a cowboy in the boat of Ra. I bedded
down with Isis, Lady of the Boogaloo, dove
down deep in her horny, stuck up her Wells-Far-ago
in daring midday get away. "Start grabbing the
blue," i said from top of my double crown.

I am a cowboy in the boat of Ra. Ezzard Charles
of the Chisholm Trail. Took up the bass but they
blew off my thumb. Alchemist in ringmanship but a
sucker for the right cross.

I am a cowboy in the boat of Ra. Vamoosed from
the temple i bide my time. The price on the wanted
poster was a-going down, outlaw alias copped my stance
and moody greenhorns were making me dance; while my
mouth's
shooting iron got its chambers jammed.

I am a cowboy in the boat of Ra. Boning-up in
the ol West i bide my time. You should see
me pick off these tin cans whippersnappers. I
write the motown long plays for the comeback of
Osiris. Make them up when stars stare at sleeping
steer out here near the campfire. Women arrive
on the backs of goats and throw themselves on
my Bowie.

I am a cowboy in the boat of Ra. Lord of the lash,
the Loup Garou Kid. Half breed son of Pisces and

Aquarius. I hold the souls of men in my pot. I do
the dirty boogie with scorpions. I make the bulls
keep still and was the first swinger to grape the taste.

I am a cowboy in his boat. Pope Joan of the
Ptah Ra. C/mere a minute willya doll?
Be a good girl and
Bring me my Buffalo horn of black powder
Bring me my headdress of black feathers
Bring me my bones of Ju-Ju snake
Go get my eyelids of red paint.
Hand me my shadow

I'm going into town after Set

I am a cowboy in the boat of Ra

look out Set   here i come Set
to get Set   to sunset Set
to unseat Set   to Set down Set

                      usurper of the Royal couch
                      imposter RAdio of Moses' bush
                      party pooper O hater of dance
                      vampire outlaw of the milky way

R I D H I A N A

Tricked Again

Come in Sweet Grief
          you foxy bastard
Liberate Romance
de-flower the Virgin
Rape the bitch

[111]

Shatter fine illusion
Ice the Expectation.

Sit down, Sweet Grief
            Saviour Lord
Sit down
            hot wine
            vodka
            lsd?
A stick of Pot
To Thee
Oh Anguish
Have a ball
            groove
Burn as Mine
My jealous own
Let your fire
Your magnificence
Riot narcotic bed ghettos.

Embrace roughly
            Grief honey
Beat, Scar, Destroy
            Shriek Outrage
Scrape four-letter
Words on House Walls
As ghosts dance
Devils chant
The Dead Rise Up
Take Love.

Then let go, Daddy
Let it go, Grief Baby
It don't hurt no more.

CONRAD KENT RIVERS

On The Death Of William Edward Burghardt Du Bois
By African Moonlight And Forgotten Shores

Truth to your mighty winds on dusky shores
    the kingdom bowed down at last,
there you were, the chosen scholar home.

True you were among the earth's unborn
    a sheik of justice and almighty intellect,
killer of liberals, brother to a distant
    universe, not easily explained to bands
of hungry black men experiencing a real truth
    spelled-out, propagated, in slums born
more vigorous each day and year of triumph,
    unemployment, wine and sweet vermouth
      squeezed against death's cool
      cocoa brown hands.

True to your souls of black folk, all hell sweeps
    our land; this moment fulfills your truths
which the State Department burned, Crisis censored,
    Marx allowed, and I see you now an old man
opening a door marked entrance, making your mark
    for the bravest party you discovered, knowing
full well that none dare give what the NAACP demands;
    but, somehow hoping your shadow fell over all
those trusting black brothers, who depend and follow
    the white's of this or any diseased land
instead of their hearts and brains and fountain pens;
    men who are ashamed to curse one another, to wail
against tyranny, power-structures, famous names,
    men against the greatness of themselves.
Sage, can there be no more hope for everyman?
    Do we walk so close to devils, lose sight of Sun,

struggle against autumnal air, quench thirst of life?
    I stand dumb and chilled to understand
        your search, your loneliness,
and my own debt for the etchings from those lonely
hills
    which now and forever hold communion over
    you.

SONIA SANCHEZ

Small Comment

the name of the beast is
man or to be more specific
the nature of man is his
bestial nature or to
bring it to its elemental terms
the nature of nature is
the bestial survival of the
fittest the strongest the richest
or to really examine
the scene we cd say that
the nature of any beast is
bestial unnatural and natural
in its struggle for superiority
and survival but to really
be with it we will say that man
is a natural beast bestial in
his lusts natural in his
bestiality and expanding
and growing on the national
scene to be the most
bestial and natural of
any beast. you dig?

JOHNIE SCOTT

The American Dream

(Part 1 of 3 parts)

"Speech, or dark cities screaming"
For a nation of illiterates
    historically unable to master
The white Man's speech
    Black People learned well.

Imprisoned in America's so-called
    Inner Cities by the Children of Yacub
One could almost hear words coming
    from the souls of Inside America.

    All Money is Is Bread!

Where there ain't no dough
    definitely there ain't no bread.
You can't eat,
    so simple it frightens it is true.

Rome wasn't burnt in a day,
    America won't burn that quickly either
Tho the desire of Yacub's Own
    historically has been to rebuild
            relive
            vaunt and flaunt
            in the faces of
            the downtrodden
            that empire built
            thru bloodied sword
            & cutting tongue.

But History is already made
    while what is future acts itself out
if not on public stage or television,
    then with the burning of modern Romes:
        Harlem
        Watts
        Detroit
        Philadelphia
        Chicago
        Newark
        Washington, D.C.
From sun-scorched rooftops
    One saw feared loved worshipped
The damn fool snipers fighting
    World War 3 with flintlocks and zip-guns.
Their pieces of iron and flint
    stroked silver streams of light
Into skies aflame with panic terror
    disbelief and pathetic heroics,
The smoke of these cities
    boggled the minds of every soldier
Firing away (sometimes indiscriminately
    always patriotically, surely justifiably).

To recapture a life-sense:
    perhaps The Supremes singing
"You Can't Hurry Love,"
    while black men women and children
Basked in the wonderment of
    very few black troopers if any at all...
Black People not in no hurry to shoot
    Black People not if the fires were for real.

The heads of bankers,
    mayors, governors, and

Presidents rolled thru
	plenty of empty bottles of Italian Swiss
	Colony White Port in that alley over there
Propelled by kicks sticks bricks
	the mob crazed by their recollections
We hold these truths
To be self-evident:
							or mirrors, of different thought/
							streams whose images caught the
							fullnesses of false beauty.
							Glinting fish that sparkled upon
							kissing with the Moon's own children:
							a sight very akin to the dismemberment
							of bastard yokels in concentration camps.

They set up Separate America
	in their own Image of Yacub's legacy:
a chestful of false prophecies,

	the Garden of Eden situated amidst the
	afterbirth of a nuclear explosion yea
	Eden itself was on fire yea God had been
	forced to summon Heaven's troops.

Nothing was holy any longer.
Families too long torn apart
Fathers wandered the streets sightless.
Stranger than all—
Fathers who did not want to see
Who would not try any longer.
Home in which
	were you able to peek as I you would know
The Family That Prays
Together Stays Together:

[117]

Homes that serve as
sources for secret chuckles...
These soulful wretches of the Earth
indistinguishable from a Hell which would
Never again be
When you see danger facing you
Little Boy don't get scared!
Its chains shattered releasing
Otis Redding's frozen body
this forgotten bluesbard a
deathwish/song, essence of Black Trial
on his lips an eternal movement:

Darlin...can't go no further now...
now that you've got me...chained and bound...

Jukeboxes long time been broken
the wax records floating in the ash-
Colored water racing down the curbs
emitting bits, flashes of light for
Those whose senses intensely caught
every motion every police car every broadcast

I've got sunshine...on a cloudy day...
when it's cold outside...I've got the month
of May

Yea, old songs old needs nevertheless
prayers from another dimension—the
Cosmos of Inner America—somehow transcending
time, disinterest, vacuities of thought

Speech, or dark cities screaming
from a dimension surpassing sensibilities

[118]

Into the Now:
> People from the Afterhere
> who understood the politics of Poverty
> knew that discussions of morality
> inevitably became political yeah
> that politics quickly turned racist,
> the most sophisticated form of wizard-
> philosophy.

Gravestones that were filled with lust
> desires aching to pour into the flesh of
Cities sans color sans Good Breeding
> bluebloods blue books as in dogs and sex-freaks

GERALD L. SIMMONS, JR.

Take Tools Our Strength...

Take tools, our strength to break chains
and locks of containment and oppression.
Look—open eyes,
see images. Black images—Beauty images,
cornbread souls and African dust.
Strike blows, death blows.
Be free.
We are beautiful,
Winners.

HERBERT A. SIMMONS

Ascendancy

Part One

1

Night grows no flower children
Though they may cuddle there.
You come like the breath of Spring
Making fertile my Indian Summer,
For I am the night star
Finding pleasure in day,
While time melts—a candle
Glowing eternal flame,
Perceiving you when you existed not,
Except in that mirror called the brain.

2

Pull tumultuous tide of people
Toward family unity,
For the key to survival is survival
And triumph, over nebulous cultures
Bent on aggrandizement and genocide.
Resides there.
Hear no siren calls of the sublime
Echoing through rundown roads of yesterday,
For today must be as tomorrow shall be,
And we must know them all.

3

We search for love in a whirlpool
Of drowning dreams disrupting days.

We find our love where the stars rule,
And blunted egos hunt for praise.

Part Two

1

Cracked blinds leaking stars in
The bedroom of affair,
In the valley of the sane,
Implanting seed of them without number.
Soar, emancipator
Discovering a way.
The high Alps — an angle,
Now shattering disdain.
Perusing a clue from the lesson taught,
And knowing the magic of a name.

2

Life hangs in the scales of the legal.
Identity with Entity.
Daybreak of love on the dawn of arrival,
Cutting through smog gifts of nutures'
Pent up ignorance stalling space ship's glide,
And no spare!
We sail our ships on the space of time.
I am that I am holding Autumn at bay,
And if climate must change at seasons decree,
There's harvest in the fall.

3

Paranoia on avenues
Of promises fools paraphrase.
We are the love that we pursue
Reflected in each other's gaze.

[121]

JOHN SINCLAIR

Breakthrough

"He who lives by the sword
        dies by the sword"

but the men who are now dying
have no such simple entrance
into their own lives—the swords they bear
(whatever "side") are *not*

what they live by, *not*
the terms of their living, but
alien & unnecessary tools
forced into their hands

by men who have taken themselves so
far from such actual simple tools that
they can now talk "rationally"
of a "minor loss" of

25 million human lives

as some abstract military feat
in a total global game of war in
which Spicer's "sole diers" are
only the most simple abstractions

Johnson, Rusk, McNamara, Westmoreland—
these are men who live by
daggers, not swords, nothing so
open as that, not that concrete

They used only *people* as their tools, & as
only that, & their game is to
set man against man, keep them
turned around like they are, at each

other's throats, screaming & killing, throwing
bricks thru windows, flying their abstract flags,
put weird abstract "names" on every
man or thing, they have gone that far

so that men are not men but a-
mericans, communists, patri-
otic, loyal, traitors, all just nomen-
clature, nomenclature. NO

MEN
clature, closing
down on us, & we are none of it but
MEN, we do have to get back to

that simple sense of our
selves, see each other as
what we are, MEN, at work at
simple human business—

getting food, making ourselves se-
cure in our homes, making such things as
poems, babies, music, houses, tools, what-
ever acts we can manage

of our lives. To get back to that
primitive a sense of it, as say the Viet-
namese people are, without blowing it
in the process, as the A-

[123]

merican people have now, & the US
soldiers have, as any of these
bloated people have here, & make a
decent life of it. To keep men simply

men, acts

acts, & have the sense somehow to
see it that way, to leave men a-
lone to them
selves, & work on it all ways

from that point, ig-
nore those others, the misled
"leaders" of this land, leave them to
atrophy & die off if they have to

& build a new life for ourselves, break
through, to where we can
live on our own, *as* our own
lovely human selves

WELTON SMITH

Strategies

i

catch him coming off the thing after a state of the union
break through all his securities with aikido
aikido a language of peace when words fail me
i make circles inside the slime of his guards
the reduction
by catching him at a moment i choose

is the reduction of security to circles
circles of big black starving eyes against
the eye of the voyeur the calculating
voyeur enthralled by the sight of pain
the pain vibrating in my own eyes—
we are face to face when the guns, the claws,
the guards tear me away
and i let them.
i am a decoy. my brothers who are all dead
shall have slipped into his head and started the long march
to his heart
which they will eat
then vomit.

ii

catch him in his lust
and chop off his brain
encircle him with my dead brothers
in his primary state he is most dangerous
he is reduced to slime and lust uncontaminated
lust and noisy wolves behind his eyes.
we are quiet, do not call it caution,
we are quieted by the language of peace
which some have not forgotten.
we move with peace close to our bodies
the peace aroused by dark eyes
aware of the texture of darkness
that has no counterpart but peace
that reduces all to circles
like circles of harmony in some pieces of music
that reduce all to quiet
when words fail.

A. B. SPELLMAN

I Looked & Saw History Caught

I looked & saw history caught
on a hinge, its two heads
like a seesaw rocking

up & down, up
& down, the eyes of the one
turned in on the Inner
College of Murder for
White Ones Especially

black & yellow beef before the
blacks of the eyes in the deathhead.
that head swings down to

ward what has been western, up
with pocketsful of shit to spread
on hectares of earth, earth
warm with the voicings of minnow
eucalyptus & cowrie, it being human

in the eye of the deathhead to people
the drumhead of history with its own
cripple progeny. thus the drumhead swings

up by the weight of death
sinking, closer to sun, grins open
to let the weather in, over clouds
of air made thick by those
opposing eyes, rotting of their own
interior commerce.
        O let that fruithead swing
        down to root, & may its shoots
        spring the sweeter past

NAZZAM AL SUDAN

Al Fitnah Muhajir

When you enter
Strange cities
Be silent
In the streets
But speak
With all
You meet
As the people see
And you will see
The poor people
Are very rich.

When you enter
Their homes
Eat with them
Or they will hate you
But eat not
That which will kill you
Even if they insist
For you have been taught
By the Great Teacher
And they know him not
May even mock him
To your face
But cool your voice
They will submit
When they meet him
When they see him
In you

When you love
Peoples of the world
Rivers are nothing
Between you
And strange tongues
A soulful tune
Salaam, salaam.

QUINCY TROUPE

White Weekend

April 5–8, 1968.

They deployed military troops
surrounded the White House
and on the steps of the Senate building
a soldier behind a machine gun

32,000 in Washington & Chicago
1900 in Baltimore Maryland
76 cities in flames on the landscape
and the bearer of peace
lying still in Atlanta...

Lamentations! Lamentations! Lamentations!
Worldwide!
But in New York, on Wall Street
the stock market went up 18 points...

DARWIN T. TURNER

Night Slivers

Night,
And Death rides fast on foul breath
belched from gaping cannon mouth.
Man dies against the sky,
ruptured by too violent peace.

Night,
On gray and carelessly-confettied street,
where bartered waters drown the stain
of siren-vanished flesh,
a child assumes a mask of white,
to mock the death-contorted mask of black.

Night,
When lonely women sell their loneliness;
men buy with breath and stones and sticks.
A girl awakens to a lie,
and knowing it a lie,
crushes it to instant's truth.

Night,
A mother stares at hidden stars
and sings to squirming life
that sucks from her dry breast.
A clean-voiced priest appeals to sightless minds
and red-necked laughs still promise patient dawn.

MALAIKA AYO WANGARA

From A Bus

Hey, little yellow boy,
You'll be better
Than me. When I came along
It was a shame to be black,
Negroes never did think black,
White was right, you see.
But listen yellow boy,
You'll be black,
Far blacker than me.

You're little now
You stand in the oversized window
With no pants on...
Where is your mother?
Your sandy hair has
A big sort of curl...
It almost looks like, well—
You know.

Who is your daddy?
     Your daddy, your mama,
     They don't see.
     They're like me.
But here you are,
Yellow you—in the heart
Of a black ghetto.

It will give you
Stinging venom to spit,
Thin lies to give,

Numberless streets to walk,
And light nights to live.
But after all these,
And they will not be long
You will be Black
And strong.
So live, yellow boy,
For your Blackness.

RON WELBURN

Regenesis

I

Growth can sit there from
a far corner
staring its years into your
brow: of thoroughfares run undulating
across the pride of nature's ebony likeness.

II

A generation in chaos
an old legion in fear
a country in terror of its shame
the sleep of past progressions endowed
in the bowels of this land.

The people behind the windows
wonder at each other
from miles apart,
wonder they why
the question they cannot

answer in articulate conception lest
those offerings blessed
by fear
spring forth unseen as harlequins are
always unseen they say.

III

Growth sits on a pane
of glass,
looking out at the seed
of decay it has shed
from itself: from
within, the seed rocks furiously
to the frenzy of a people
caught in revolution.

JOHN A. WILLIAMS

Safari West

The South Atlantic clouds rode low
in the sky; blue-fringed with rain that
would come later.
Popo Channel ran strong beneath its mud-green
undulating surface and the boatmen pointed
and told me
there were barracudas there. They swam in
from the ocean side, just to take a look,
hoping, perhaps
that slavery had returned and rebellious
and sick and dying blacks were being dumped
into the waters again.

Badagry, the town roofed over with rusted
tin and walled concrete hard mud, peddles a
view of its baracoon.
For a Nigerian pound; for two you can heft
old irons worn thin and trod the cells.
Ah, God!
Chains for the rebellious, the old, the strong;
chains for the weak, the children, all westbound,
all black.
And I raised each crude instrument to places
where gone, gone brothers had worn them,
the ankles,
wrists, necks, and mouths, and did not wipe
my lips, hoping some terribly dormant
all-powerful
Germ of saliva would dart quickly within
and shock awake memory, fury, wisdom
and retribution.
It did. And Nigerians drowsed in the heat
or floated through it, their voices truly
musical,
and wondered at this black man clothed in
the cloth of the West, his eyes swinging
angrily
out over Popo Island and beyond, West,
West to the Middle Passage, eyes swinging
with wet anger.
There is an old one-pounder in the village;
it stands where a missionary, prelude to
Western armies
once had a church. When the ships rounded
Popo and stood swollen in the channel,
the missionary,
Forgetful of his role, fired the cannon to

warn his flock that the slavers had come.
Again.
As the vessels rode high in the channel
with light cargoes of cloth, trinkets and other
Western waste and
lowered their sails in the humid wind,
the blacks ran and traitors ran with them
deep into the bush.
They could not run fast or far enough or fear
quite enough. The Badagry baracoon stand
today,
somewhat maintained, I think, in the manner
in which Dachau is maintained in something of
greater degree.

A L Y O U N G

A Dance For Ma Rainey

I'm going to be just like you, Ma
Rainey this monday morning
clouds puffing up out of my head
like those balloons
that float above the faces of white people
in the funnypapers

I'm going to hover in the corners
of the world, Ma
& sing from the bottom of hell
up to the tops of high heaven
& send out scratchless waves of yellow
& brown & that basic black honey
misery

I'm going to cry so sweet
& so low
& so dangerous,
Ma,
that the message is going to reach you
back in 1922
where you shimmer
snaggle-toothed
perfumed &
powdered
in your bauble beads
hair pressed & tied back
throbbing with that sick pain
I know
& hide so well
that pain that blues
jives the world with
aching to be heard
that downness
that bottomlessness
first felt by some stolen delta nigger
swamped under with redblooded american agony;
reduced to the sheer shit
of existence
that bred
& battered us all,
Ma,
the beautiful people
our beautiful people
our beautiful brave black people
who no longer need to jazz
or sing to themselves in murderous vibrations
or play the veins of their strong tender arms
with needles
to prove how proud we are

[135]

STATEMENTS ON POETICS

STATEMENTS ON POETICS

DON L. LEE: "Black art is created from black forces that live within the body....Direct and meaningful contact with black people will act as energizers for the black forces....We must destroy Faulkner, dick, jane and other perpetuators of evil. It's time for Du Bois, Nat Turner, and Kwame Nkrumah."

CHARLES F. GORDON: "I am black because I am Black; everything I write, poems and stories, will be black without any artificial strain."

NAZAM AL SUDAN: "I believe the style of our poetry is but a reflection of our life-style. The form of a poem depends on the form of our life, how we live. The form or logic of a poem reflects our maturity or immaturity, our personal perfection or imperfection. What we want to do, most of all, in our poetry (and in our interpersonal relations) is to say precisely what is on our minds....The poet's job is to help the people talk better—to help the people live better. Of course, the first person the poem ought to help is the poet."

QUENTIN HILL: "Black words do not exist in this country apart from the minds and voices of black people. The ritual of transubstantiation (the power of word [magic; *nommo*]), the changing of white words to black ones, does not function passively. A book of black poetry cannot be bought, it is only through the action of book and mind that the poems contained in them (both book and mind) attain a state that could be called *black*. Only through utterance (vocal or mental) do words achieve their natural state.

"The function of our poetry parallels the function of our music: (extensions of the voice), both give motion back to

[139]

the people...the difference between black music and black poetry seems to be that black music is a product of the creative faculties of a black individual who reorganizes all of his perceptions to express himself, while black poetry depends on the predicament of black people living here. The music utilizes all perception, black poetry only the perceptions which directly and collectively relate to the mass of black people....

"The purpose of black poetry is to evoke response in its audience, the black masses, since ideally it is the mass of black people who are speaking. The response evoked must lead to change whether that change be immediate or proceeding over an undetermined period of time....I hope to wake up one morning in a land where I can write anything I want to, for part of the creative process is choosing what one wants to create rather than creating what one has to."

CONRAD KENT RIVERS: "It is only through our exploitation of our experience that our vision and our ventures will ring true for the literate. ...If we fail to write for black people, we—in effect—fail to write at all."

JULIA FIELDS: "In the future, the only relevant literature will be that which has gone directly to the heart of Blackness....The black experience seems the most intense experience in the modern world. It is better that black people write it ourselves rather than have it written for us exploitatively."

S. E. ANDERSON: "We are an oppressed people. What is therefore needed is a revolution. A revolution of self, family, society, nation, values, culture. The black writer must necessarily aid in the liberation struggle....He must help black people....In the process of directing his work toward black people, he is creating a new man, a new humanism."

[140]

LARRY NEAL: "Essentially, art is relevant when it makes you stronger. That is, the only thing which is fundamental to good art is its ritual quality. And the function of ritual is to reinforce the group's operable myths, ideals, and values. The oldest, most important arts, have always made their practitioners stronger. Here I refer to the Black Arts, ju-ju, voodoo, and the Holy Ghost of the Black Church. The black Arts are among the earliest examples of mixed media. They combined ritualistic drama, music, the poetry of incantation, and the visual arts. The intent was to communicate with the Spirit. The ritual act served to make the participants stronger....

"We are Black writers (priests), the bearers of the ancient tribal tradition. Only we have lived in the West: and we must understand what that experience means. And we must confront that experience as Black men first. As writers, one of our sacred functions is to reconstruct our ancient tradition and to give that tradition meaning in light of the manner in which history has moved....Culturally and artistically, the West is dead. We must understand that we are what's happening. After so many years of enforced silence, the oppressed everywhere on this planet are beginning to tell their version of the story of Man....I have written 'love' poems that act to liberate the soul as much as any 'war' poem I have written."

ETHERIDGE KNIGHT: "The Caucasian has separated the aesthetic dimension from all others, in order that undesirable conclusions might be avoided. The artist is encouraged to speak only of the beautiful...his task is to edify the listener, to make him see *beauty* of the world. And this is the trick bag that Black Artists must avoid, because the red of this aesthetic rose got its color from the blood of black slaves, exterminated Indians, napalmed Vietnamese children, etc., *ad nauseum....*When the white aesthetic does permit the artist to speak of ugliness and evil—and this is the biggest trick in the whole bag—the ugliness and evil must be a 'universal human condition,' a flimflam justification for the continuous enslavement of the world's colored peoples. The white aesthetic would tell the Black Artist that *all* men have the same problems, that they all try to find their dignity and identity."

ELTON HILL-ABU ISHAK: "We are calling for all black people to come to terms with their minds. We do not want a blk santa clause or a blk peter pan. We want change not a white society painted blk."

SAM CORNISH: "I try to put down the things I can see in a way people can understand."

JUNE MEYER: "Poetry is an exact transliteration of reality and dreams into new reality and into new dreams. Poetry is the most precise use of words because it is most particular, intense and brief. Poetry is the way I think and the way I remember and the way I understand or the way I express my confusion, bitterness and love....Poetry challenges the apparent respectability of abstractions by offering a completely particular statement of a completely particular event whether the event is a human being or the response of one human being to poverty, for example."

The statements by Rivers, Fields, Neal and Knight are excerpted from Negro Digest, *January 1968.*

BIOGRAPHICAL SKETCHES

BIOGRAPHICAL SKETCHES

S.E. ANDERSON: Born 1943; received an AB in Mathematics from Lincoln University. His works have appeared in *The Liberator, Negro Digest,* and *Soulbook.* Anderson is co-editor of *Mojo,* the important black student organ. He teaches math and is working toward his masters at City College, New York City. "A New Dance" is from manuscript.

RUSSELL ATKINS: Born 1926; attended Cleveland Institute of Music and Music Settlement, but later turned to creative theory and invented the composing technique of Psychovisualism, introduced at the 1956 Festival of Contemporary Music, Germany. He edits *Free Lance,* from Cleveland. His poem in this volume was originally published in that magazine (1962).

LAURENCE BENFORD: Born 1946 in Texas; presently an under-graduate at Pan American College, Edinburg, Texas, with a major in English and philosophy. He has published in several magazines including *American Bard.* "The Beginning Of A Long Poem On Why I Burned The City" is from manuscript.

LEBERT BETHUNE: Born 1937 in Kingston, Jamaica; after obtaining a BS from New York University he studied in France. Aside from his poetry, he has written and co-edited two Court-Metrage documentary films. Has published several articles, plays and a novel, *Skate's Dive.* "To Strike For Night" is from his book of poems, *A Juju Of My Own* (1966).

HART LEROI BIBBS: Born 1930 in Kansas City, Mo.; attended New York University to study journalism and creative writing. His poems have appeared in several publications such as *Liberator* and *Kauri.* His poem "Six Sunday" is from his book *Poly-Rhythms To Freedom* (1964).

AUSTIN BLACK: Born 1928 in East St. Louis, Ill.; works as a photo journalist with commercial outlets such as *Jet, Sepia, Teen Time.* He published a book of poems, *A Tornado in My Mouth* (Exposition, 1966). "Soul" is from manuscript.

EDWIN BROOKS: Born 1928 in Toledo, Ohio; attended the university there. "My dead aunt, Anna Lee Davis, who was not able to go beyond 6th grade, always encouraged me—her relatives—to go to school and read and study. I shall always love her. I want my people to be free." "Tulips From Their Blood" is from manuscript.

F.J. BRYANT: Born 1942 in Philadelphia, Penna.; graduated from Lincoln University in 1967. His work also appears in the anthology, *Blackfire.* "The Languages We Are" is from manuscript.

ED BULLINS: Born 1935 in Philadelphia, Penna. His many one-act plays have received much critical and popular attention on both coasts. His stories, essays, and poems have been published in *Illuminations, Wild Dog,* and many other *avant garde* magazines as well as in all the black literary quarterlies. Three of his plays had a successful run during the Spring of 1968, first at the American Place Theatre and later at the Martinique Theatre, in New York. "When Slavery Seems Sweet" appeared in the *Journal Of Black Poetry* (1967).

LEN CHANDLER: Born 1935 in Akron, Ohio; attended the University of Ohio and received his MA from Columbia University in New York. A poet and concert vocalist, his records are released by Columbia. He is a frequent guest on radio and TV. "I Would Be A Painter Most Of All" appeared in *Umbra* (1967).

SAM CORNISH: Born 1938 in West Baltimore, Md.; edits the poetry magazine, *Mimeo.* Among the various paperback volumes of his poems are: *People Under The Window, In This Corner,* and *The Shabby Breath of Yellow Teeth.* In 1968 he was awarded the prize for poetry by the Humanities Institute, Coppin State College, as well as a grant from the National Endowment of the Arts. "To A Single Shadow" is from manuscript.

STANLEY CROUCH: Born 1945; his poetry has appeared in numerous publications including the anthology *Black Fire.* He was contracted by Harper & Row to finish his novel, *The Music;* columnist for the *Los Angeles Free Press* and the *Cricket.* Is Arts Coordinator of Cultural Afternoons at Watts Happening Coffee House, and a playwright/actor, with the Watts Repertory Theatre Co. "Chops Are Flying" is from manuscript.

[146]

VICTOR HERNANDEZ CRUZ: Born 1949 in Aguas Buenas, Puerto Rico; moved to New York City, 1952. His poems have appeared in *Evergreen, Umbra, For Now, Down Here,* and others. Random House is to publish a volume of his poems, *Snaps.* He recently opened the *Gut-Theatre,* in East Harlem. "Urban Dream" is from manuscript.

GLORIA DAVIS: A young poet of Detroit; published in *Uhuru* and other magazines. The poem, "Theme Brown Girl" by Elton Hill-Abu Ishak in this anthology is for her. "To Egypt" is from manuscript.

RAY DUREM: Born 1915; veteran of the Spanish Civil War, who died in 1963. He was widely published during his lifetime. Though a collection of his poems is being compiled, there is no way to measure the depth of artistic perfection this extremely skillful poet might have achieved had he lived 48 years more. "Problem In Social Geometry" is from *Umbra* (1967).

HARRY EDWARDS: Born 1942, in St. Louis, Mo.; currently a Professor of Sociology at Cornell University, New York; political activist and organizer of the 1968 Olympics Boycott. (His poem is a "found poem" put together by Walter Lowenfels from an Edwards quote in the *New York Times.*)

JULIA FIELDS: Born 1938 in Uniontown, Ala.; received a BS degree from Knoxville College (1961); was in residence at the Breadloaf Writers' Conference, Middlebury, in 1962. Her poems have appeared in *Massachussetts Review, Riverside Poetry 11, Beyond the Blues, New Negro Poets, American Negro Poetry.* "Black Students" is from *Negro Digest* (1967).

BOB FLETCHER: Born 1938 in Detroit, Mich.; attended Fisk University, Nashville. Aside from poetry, he worked as a SNCC communications director. "A Love Dirge To The Whitehouse Or (It Soots You Right)" is from *Umbra* (1967).

NIKKI GIOVANNI: Born 1943 in Knoxville, Tenn.; has published prose and poetry in various magazines and has to her credit a collection of poems, *Black Feeling* (1968). "I'd like to have mentioned that I was kicked out of Fisk, plus I dropped out of a Masters Program at the University of Pennsylvania. And I was in love once." "Nikki Roasa" is from manuscript.

CHARLES F. GORDON: Born 1943 in Lorain, Ohio; attended Miami University in Oxford, Ohio, and New York University. He has published in *Mojo, The Oxford Free Press* and elsewhere. He edits the magazine *Gumbo* from Harlem. "The Long Night Home" is from manuscript.

DONALD D. GOVAN: Born 1945 in Minot, N. Dak. His mother is a Turtle Mountain Indian and his father a black man from Texas. He grew up on various reservations; has danced with an Indian dancing troupe, worked as a shoe shine boy while attending St. Cloud State University, where he began studying literature until he was imprisoned (1967) in Sandstone Federal Correctional Institution "for not paying the tax on grass." Govan plans to continue his formal education and creative writing when he is released. "Recollection" is from manuscript.

CAROLE GREGORY: A young poet of Youngstown, Ohio, who recently graduated from that state's university with an AB in English. "Glad to know you're concerned about the brothers and sisters in poetry writing." "Ghetto Lovesong—Migration" is from manuscript.

JOHN HALL: Born 1943 in Cleveland, Ohio; has read his poems with the Muntu Workshop at Community College's Diogenes, Lantern and CORE's Target City Festival during Black Arts Week. "Dark Shadows" is from manuscript.

ALBERT HAYNES: Born 1936 in Kingston, Jamaica; worked with the original *Umbra* group, and is also a painter, who lives on Long Island, New York. "The Law" is from manuscript.

DAVID HENDERSON: Born 1942 in Harlem, New York. He attended Hunter College and the New School for Social Research, both in New York. His poems have appeared in numerous publications and important anthologies. His collection of poems, *Felix of the Silent*

Forest (The Poets Press, 1967) was introduced by LeRoi Jones. "Psychadelic Firemen" is from manuscript.

CALVIN C. HERNTON: Born 1933 in Chattanooga, Tenn.; educated at Southern Negro colleges—Talladega, Ala., and Fisk; and later at Columbia University. His book of poetry is entitled *The Coming of Chronos to the House of Nightsong.* His other books include; *Sex and Racism in America* (1965), and *White Papers for White Americans* (1966). He taught at the Antiuniversity of London (Summer, 1968). "Elements Of Grammar" is from manuscript.

QUENTIN HILL: Born 19 years ago in the South Bronx, N.Y.C.; a student at New York University. "I grew up in a housing project where the only white families were as poor as mine and so I didn't learn first hand about cracker treachery until Jr. H.S. Everything fell into place during the Harlem riot of '64 which I did as much to start as anyone else....After that I began to act like a black male rather than a poor kid." "Time Poem" is from manuscript.

EVERETT HOAGLAND: Born 1942 in Philadelphia, Penna.; graduated from Lincoln University, Penna., in 1964, with a creative writing award. Completed graduate school and is currently Assistant Director of Admissions at Lincoln. His recent work *Ten Poems* is published by the American Studies Institute. "Night Interpreted" is from manuscript.

ELTON HILL-ABU ISHAK: Born 1950 in Detroit, Mich. He is the editor of *Uhuru: The Freedom Magazine,* and has published in a number of magazines. "Theme Brown Girl (For Gloria)" appeared in *Uhuru* (1968).

LANCE JEFFERS: Born 1919 in Fremont, Neb.; holds an honors degree from Columbia University; has taught college English. A short story of his appeared in the 1948 *The Best American Short Stories.* His poems have appeared in *Tamarack Review,* in the anthologies, *Burning Spear* and *Beyond the Blues.* Now an assistant Professor of English, teaching creative writing at California State College. "My Blackness Is The Beauty Of This Land" appeared in *Desein* (1966).

ALICIA L. JOHNSON: Born 1944 in Chicago, Ill.; attended Wilson Junior College, and is presently enrolled at Southern Illinois University. Her works have appeared in many publications, including *Negro Digest, Journal of Black Poetry,* and *Black Expressions.* "Black Lotus/a prayer" is from *The Journal Of Black Poetry* (1968).

HOWARD JONES: Born 1941 in New York City; he began writing in the Air Force, 1959-63, while stationed atop a thousand-foot high cliff overlooking nothing. His work has appeared in *Uptown Beat,* from which "Fall T^O" was taken (1968).

LEROI JONES: Born 1934 in Newark, N.J.; attended Rutgers, Columbia and Howard Universities, and the New School (NYC); awarded a Guggenheim fellowship (1964-65). His best-known play, *Dutchman,* was awarded the Obie for the best off-Broadway play of 1963-64. He has published three collections of poems, six plays, two collections of articles, a novel, a volume of short stories, and other works. Jones was the founder and director of the Black Arts Repertory Theatre/School in Harlem (1964). He now directs Spirit House in Newark.

NORMAN JORDAN: Born 1938 in Ansted, W. Va.; his poems appear in *Blackfire,* and other anthologies. He has recently worked with students at the Muntu Workshop, Cleveland. "Feeding The Lions" was published several times in small circulating publications.

BOB KAUFMAN: A young poet who first became identified with the Beat Generation, continues to live in San Francisco; author of *Solitudes Crowded With Loneliness* (New Directions, 1965) and *Golden Sardine* (City Lights, 1967). His works have also frequently appeared in many San Francisco-oriented poetry magazines and anthologies. Incidentally, he is better known in Europe than here.

ETHERIDGE KNIGHT: Born 1933 in Corinth, Miss.; his poems appear in *Negro Digest, The Goliards,* and elsewhere and his short stories in *Prison* Magazine, *Negro Digest,* and *Jaguar.* He received a prison sentence in 1960 and writes from Indiana State Prison. "He Sees Through Stone" is from *Black Dialogue* (1967).

[150]

DON L. LEE: "I was born into slavery in Feb., of 1942.... " Author of *Think Black* (Broadside) and *Black Pride* (Broadside), he has also published in *Evergreen, The Journal of Black Poetry* and other magazines. He teaches at Roosevelt University in Chicago. "Re-Act For Action" is from *Black Pride* (1968).

CY LESLIE: Born 1921 in St. Croix, Virgin Islands; received degree of Doctor of Dental Surgery at Meharry Medical College, is also a photographer and sculptor. "On Riots" is from *Journal of Black Poetry* (1968).

WORTH LONG: Born 1936 in Durham, N.C.; former Staff Coordinator of SNCC. His poems have appeared in *Le Poésie Negro Americaine, Harvard Advocate,* and the *New South.* "Arson and Cold Lace" is from *Umbra* (1967).

AUDRE LORDE: Born 1934 in New York City; attended Hunter College, received her masters from Columbia and spent a year at the University of Mexico. Was poet-in-residence at Tougaloo College last spring. "What My Child Learns Of The Sea" is from her book of poems, *First Cities* (Poets Press, 1968).

JOSEPH MAJOR: Born 1948 in Brooklyn, N.Y. "I believe in a thousand different kinds of love, and am fairly convinced that no law whatsoever has ever touched on happiness." He is a student, and lives in New York. "Poem For Thel—The Very Tops Of Trees" is from manuscript.

JUNE MEYER: Born 1936 in Harlem, N.Y.; attended Northfield School for Girls, Barnard College and University of Chicago. Aside from writing poetry she writes criticism, teaches at the college level, and is editing an anthology of poems for children. "All The World Moved" is from manuscript.

ERNIE MKALIMOTO: Born Ernest Allen, 1942 in California; attended Merritt College, Oakland, and University of California at Berkeley. After a visit to Cuba in 1964, when he met "Che" Guevara, he worked for several black political projects, helped to form the House of Umoja. "Energy For A New Thang" appeared in *Soulbook* (1967).

JOSEPH M. MOSLEY JR.: Born 1935 in Philadelphia; attended the Catholic Church Monastery but renounced Roman Catholicism in 1966. His poetry has appeared in several publications such as *Freedomways*. "Black Church On Sunday" is from manuscript.

GLENN MYLES: Born 1933 in Carthage, Texas; has written and lectured on art and contemporary problems. Published design and illustration in various outlets, such as *Esquire* and KPFA radio. He wrote from Paris. "Percy 68" appeared in *Uhuru* (1968).

LARRY NEAL: Born 1937 in Atlanta, Ga. Graduated from Lincoln University in 1961; did post-graduate study at University of Pennsylvania. His poetry, literary and social criticism have appeared in many magazines and books. "Orishas" is from *Journal Of Black Poetry* (1968).

MICHAEL NICHOLAS: Born 1941 in Mobile, Ala.; holds a BA in Slavic Languages from Los Angeles City College and a MA in Linguistics from University of Hawaii. He published a collection of poems *Watermellons into Wine* (1968). "Today; The Idea Market" is from manuscript.

DT OGILVIE: Wrote from Washington, D.C.: "I am a new author and have not been published before." "Last Letter To The Western Civilization" is from manuscript.

CHARLES PATTERSON: Born 1941 in Red Springs, N.C.; a playwright as well as a poet. His plays have been produced by several Off-Off Broadway theaters. "Listen" appeared in *Umbra* (1967).

RAY PATTERSON: Born 1929, in New York City; supports himself by teaching. His work has appeared in *For Malcolm* (Broadside), *Beyond the Blues*, and elsewhere. He has read his poetry in many places in New York.

TOM POOLE: Born 1938 in Ashville, N.C.; "Occupation: practicing psychotic." Actually, he works as a research analyst. Has traveled widely and kept detailed personal journals. Now lives in New York. "I Wonder" is from manuscript.

N.H. PRITCHARD: Born 1939 in New York; attended Washington Square College, Institute of Fine Arts, Columbia University, and New York University. Has published in *Poetry Northwest, Liberator, East Village Other, Negro Digest.* He is also included in the record album, *Destinations: Four Contemporary American Poets,* and in Walter Lowenfels' album, *New Jazz Poets* (Folkways). "Metagnomy" is from manuscript.

HELEN QUIGLESS: Born 1944 in Washington, D.C.; attended Putney School, Vermont, Bard College and Fisk University, where she received a BA in English. Her work has appeared in *For Malcolm, The Fisk Herald,* and elsewhere. She studied writing under John Oliver Killens and Robert Hayden. "Concert" is from manuscript.

DUDLEY RANDALL: Born 1914 in Washington, D.C.; received a BA in English from Wayne University, 1945, and a MA from University of Michigan, 1951. He is the editor and publisher of the Broadside Press, Detroit. "Blackberry Sweet" is from manuscript.

LENNOX RAPHAEL: Born 1940 in Trinidad, West Indies; worked as a reporter in Jamaica. His prose and poetry have been published in *American Dialog* and *Negro Digest,* and he is a staff writer for the *East Village Other* newspaper. "Infants Of Summer" is from manuscript.

AMIR RASHIDD: Born 1943 in Cleveland, Ohio, where he is a charter member of the Muntu Workshop. Participated in the Black Arts festivals and conventions sponsored by BSU. "Eclipse" is from manuscript.

NIEMA RASHIDD: A young poet, born Niema Fuller, who lives in Detroit, and edits the magazine, *A Time For Prophecy.* "Warriors Prancing, Women Dancing...." originally appeared in its pages (1968).

EUGENE REDMOND: His poems have appeared in various magazines and newspapers and he has won several prizes for poetry. He is a Teacher-Counselor at Southern Illinois University's Experiment in Higher Education. "Gods In Vietnam" is from manuscript.

ISHMAEL REED: Born 1938, in Chattanooga, Tenn.; attended University of Buffalo. His first novel, *The Free-Lance Pallbearers* (Doubleday, 1967) has been reprinted and translated. He was one of the founders of the *East Village Other* newspaper. "I Am A Cowboy In The Boat Of Ra" is from manuscript.

RIDHIANA: Attended Ohio State University, where she received a BA from the School of Journalism in 1959. Did graduate work at UCLA and USC. "Current phase finds me working outside the system to publish the *Uprising* News Magazine..." "Tricked Again" is from manuscript.

CONRAD KENT RIVERS: Born 1933 in Atlantic City, N.J., and died July 1967 in Gary, Ind.; attended Wilberforce University. He taught high school English in Gary. His poems have appeared in *Kenyon Review*, *Antioch Review*, *Free Lance*, *American Negro Poetry*, and other magazines. His books of poetry include *These Black Bodies* and *This Sunburnt Face*. "On The Death Of William Edward Burghardt Du Bois..." first appeared in *Free Lance* (1967).

SONIA SANCHEZ: Born 1935 in Birmingham, Ala.; attended New York University and took her BA at Hunter College (1955). Her poems have appeared in *Transatlantic Review*, *Minnesota Review*, *New England Review*, *Afro-American Festival of the Arts*, *For Malcolm*, etc. Currently teaching creative writing at San Francisco State College, under Black Studies. "Small Comment" is from manuscript.

JOHNIE SCOTT: Born 1946 in Watts, Los Angeles. He has been published widely, including *Harpers*, *Time*, *Pageant*, *Negro Digest*, *The Burning Bush*, *Uhuru*. Also has two NBC "Experiments in Television" to his credit. Formerly was with Bud Schulberg's Watts Writer's Workshop. He is Director of Affairs, Afro-West; Theatre of the Black Arts; also presently attending Stanford University. "The American Dream" is from manuscript.

GERALD L. SIMMONS, Jr.: Born 1944 in Memphis, Tenn. A professional photographer, co-chairman of the Black Students Union, Wayne State University, Detroit. "Take Tools Our Strength. . . ." appeared in *Uhuru* (1968).

HERBERT A. SIMMONS: Born 1930 in St. Louis, Mo.; attended Washington University there, and received a BA degree in 1958; did graduate work on a Writers Workshop Fellowship at University of Iowa; received a Sara B. Glasglow Award 1956 for *The Stranger,* a play; the Houghton-Mifflin Literary Award for *Corner Boy,* a novel. His second novel, *Man Walking On Eggshells,* was published in 1962. He is presently involved in co-ordinating the Original Watts Writers Workshop and in the formation of an all-black communications media industry called *Watts 13,* in L.A. "Ascendancy" is from manuscript.

JOHN SINCLAIR: Born 1941 in Flint, Mich.; studied at Albion College and received BA in 1964 from University of Michigan; graduate work at Wayne State University. His work has appeared in *el corno emplumado, Work, Poems Now, Jazz, It, Out of Sight, Spero, Change, Arts & Artists.* His books of poetry include *This Is Our Music* (1965), *The Leni Poems,* (1966), *Bridgework* (1967). Has also written for *Downbeat, Coda, Sounds & Fury, Kulchur, New University Thought,* and other magazines. "Breakthrough" is from his collection of poems *Firemusic* (1966).

WELTON SMITH: Born in Houston, Texas; has published in several magazines, including *Black Dialogue* (1968), from which "Strategies" is taken.

A.B. SPELLMAN: Born 1936 in Nixonton, N.C.: BA in Political Science and History from Howard University. He has published in many magazines and his books include *The Beautiful Days* (Poets Press), and *Four Lives In The Bebop Business* (Pantheon). He is currently Writer-in-residence at Moorehouse College Atlanta.

NAZZAM AL SUDAN: Born 1944 in Fowles, Cal.; attended Oakland City College, from which he received a degree in sociology. He is the author of the play, *Flowers For The Whiteman* or *Take Care of Business.* "I am presently somewhere in the Third World fighting for freedom, justice and equality among our own kind on some of this good earth that we can call our own." "Al Fitnah Muhajir" is from manuscript.

QUINCY TROUPE: Born 1943 in New York City; attended Grambling College, La., and Los Angeles City College. He has published in many magazines, including *Antioch Review, Inside Story, Miscellaneous Man*. He teaches Black History at the Watts Writers Workshop, L.A. "White Weekend" is from manuscript.

DARWIN T. TURNER: Born 1931 in Cincinnati, Ohio; graduated Phi Beta Kappa from University of Cincinnati with a BA in English; MA from the same school and a Ph.D from the University of Chicago. He is presently a Professor of English and Dean of Graduate School at North Carolina. He has published a study-guide to the novel, *The Scarlet Letter*. A book of his poems is titled, *Katharsis*. "Night Slivers" is from manuscript.

MALAIKA AYO WANGARA: Born Joyce Whitsitt, 1938, in Mount Clemens, Detroit; attended Western Michigan University in Kalamazoo, and Wayne State University in Detroit; teaches for a living. Has published in several contemporary black magazines as well as the *Negro History Bulletin*. "From A Bus" appeared in the *Journal Of Black Poetry* (1968).

RON WELBURN: Born 1944 in Bryn Mawr, Penna.; BA from Lincoln University. He published in John Sinclair's *Guerrilla* newspaper and other Detroit Artists Workshop Press publications. "Regenesis" is from manuscript.

JOHN A. WILLIAMS: Born in Jackson, Miss., 1925 and attended University of Syracuse; lives in New York City. A collection of his poems is titled simply, *Poems;* other books are *The Angry Black, Beyond The Angry Black, Night Song, Sissie, This Is My Country Too, The Man Who Cried I Am. Night Song*, under another title, was made into a movie, staring Dick Gregory. "Safari West" is from manuscript.

AL YOUNG: Born 1939, in Ocean Springs, Miss.; attended University of Michigan and University of California at Berkeley. Has worked as a professional musician and at innumerable day jobs in San Francisco. He was awarded a Wallace E. Stegner Creative Writing Fellowship by Stanford University, 1966-67. Edits *Loveletter*, a magazine in the mimeo-revolution. "A Dance For Ma Rainey" appeared in the *Journal of Black Poetry* (1968).